I Support Her

GIVNG A VOICE TO THE UNHEARD STORIES FROM
INCREDIBLE WOMEN

I SUPPORT HER

Copyright © 2020 Caged Bird Publishing

All rights reserved.

All rights reserved. No part of this book may be reproduced or used in any manner without the written permission of the copyright owner except for the use of quotations in a book review.

ISBN: 978-1-7341820-2-6 paperback
ISBN: 978-1-7341820-3-3 eBook

Photographer: Joseph Kelly
Cover Model: Tyisha McCoy
Cover Concept and Graphic Design: Danielle Ferreira

Foreword written by: Award Winning Author Vernard VDOR Dorsey

Prologue written by: Rebekah Hill

Published by: Caged Bird Publishing
www.cagedbirdpublishing.com

DEDICATION

This Book is Dedicated to Mr. Kenneth Elliot Linden Millington; not only was he a friend a brother and a shipmate, he was Caged Bird Publishing's biggest fan. Thank you for all your support, encouragement and honesty. Fair wind and following seas! Rest in Heaven!

April 27, 1975 -July 11, 2020

FOREWORD

In a time and era of not only "Times up" and the "Me too" movements, the calls for racial and gender equality and equal rights has never been more apparent. Far too often, we as men take for granted what it means to fill the shoes of our female counterparts. Not only thorough the burdens of being a mother, a wife, and often a single parent, while enduring menstrual cycles, postpartum and menopause, but the daily struggles of being viewed as sex symbols, told they're not smart enough, preyed upon and used as a lucrative means of income by way of prostitution, or belittled by way of unequal pay and unequal opportunity in the workplace. As the nurturers of our existence and the backbone of our success, we as men and as a society "have to do better" in appreciating what a woman brings to the table.

In the midst of these trying times, I salute the bravery and courage of these ten women, who've come forward to share their painful stories, to remind us of the struggles, and challenges they face for simply being who they are…a woman. Through your pain of being homeless, your pain of sexual abuse, your pain of physical abuse, your pain of losing a child, your pain of losing a mother, your pain of alcoholism, your pain of recovering from cancer, your pain of false imprisonment, your pain of mental illness – ladies, we hear you. Yet, for many men as we become bread winners, dominate in the bedroom, climb the ladder of success, and become masters of the universe – we tend to forget that the women we disregard and take for granted, represent the same gender as our own precious mothers. For this, I am sorry. I apologize for how we as men become so involved in ourselves – lost in our own egos and bravado – that we often lose sight of what's most important…our significant others.

From a personal perspective, unfortunately, I was raised in an environment where verbal abuse, physical abuse, and womanizing was an all too familiar way of life growing up. Despite my personal pledge to never perpetuate these behaviors, when I came of age, I too have fallen a time or two to the abrasiveness of my upbringing. However, through maturity and decency, I've owned my indiscretions and acknowledge my faults by saying, "we can do better, we can be better." I say all this to say that, although no mortal man is perfect. We *all* harness the ability to be the best version of ourselves and do right by these same women who bear our children and coddle us as men as we face our own challenges when life is not treating us kind. Again, "we can do better."

Until then, to all the daughters, mothers, grandmothers, wives, fiancées, and significant others of the world, as you continue to endure the hardships of life personally and socially, I admire your strength and encourage you to continue your quest to fight for your equality, claim your independence, fight against your injustice, and take the power back from all of life's adversities.

I SUPPORT HER

Whether you're a woman who shared your testimony in this book, or any woman enduring the tribulations of everyday life. No matter what your struggle may look like, just know that "I Support Her!"

~*Vdor*

By the Author, Buy the Book!

CONTENTS

DEDICATION iv
FOREWORD v
CONTENTS viii
ACKNOWLEDGMENTS 1
PROLOGUE 2
CHAPTER 1 4
Molestation, Money and Family 4
"Who knew this would be my life." 4
By: Kaleta Green 4
CHAPTER 2 37
A Mother's Ordeal 37
"Dealing with Breast Cancer...My Own Way,"! 37
By: Gloria Jean Eason 37
CHAPTER 3 67
From The Pit to Promise 67
"My Journey from Homelessness to Home" 67
by: Kenesa Bowe 67
CHAPTER 4 124
Hidden Sentence 124
"No One Prepares You for Coming Home" 124
By: Pamela O'Hara 124
CHAPTER 5 135

The Box on the Shelf 135
"Surviving Unspeakable Loss" 135
By: Danielle Ferreira 135

CHAPTER 6 159
Her Bleeding Heart Made Whole Again 159
"If God Saved Me, He Can Save You" 159
By: Albertina Dancy 159

CHAPTER 7 166
Body Count Zero 166
"Surviving Cervical Cancer" 166
By: Tiffanie Davis Shelton 166

CHAPTER 8 181
Beauty For Ashes 181
"Recovery from Childhood Trauma" 181
By: Tyishua McCoy 181

CHAPTER 9 206
For My Good but For His Glory 206
"Coming Up The Rough Side Of The Mountain" 206
By: Tabisha AnnQuaneete McCoy 206

CHAPTER 10 214
Return to Sobriety 214
"Surviving to Thriving" 214
By: Toni Ferguson 214

ABOUT THE AUTHORS 232

ACKNOWLEDGMENTS

Immeasurable appreciation and deepest gratitude are extended to the following persons who, in one way or another, have contributed in making this anthology possible. This book would be nothing without the hard work and dedication of all the wonderful co-authors. Thank you for your willingness to open yourself up to the world. May God continue to bless your journey.

Special Thanks:

Author Vernard "Vdor" Dorsey
IPPY Award-Winning Author, 5-Star Rated Writer, Inventor, Engineer and USCG (Ret)
https://www.vdorauthor.com/

Mr. Kenneth Williams
WPCE 1400 Christian Broadcasting Co.
www.WPCE1400.com

Joseph Kelly
Freelance Photographer
https://www.Lilysnbloomstudios.com

Karen Stallings
CEO Colour U Cosmetics Inc
https://www.muapromakeupartistryacademy.com/

Rebekah S. Hill
Assistant Editor

Again, WE thank you!

Sincerely,
Danielle Ferreira C.E.O, Caged Bird Publishing

PROLOGUE

Father God,

I come before You thankful. Thanking You for the lives of the women who have so transparently shared their experiences in this anthology. I thank You for Your faithfulness in bringing them thru situations that, in the natural eye, seemed like tragedy; circumstances that, without You, would have been impossible.

But You kept them, and for that, I am grateful. Thank You for Your guidance when we have no idea which way to go, Your strength when we feel we cannot take not even one more step, and Your mercy to pick us back up and tend to us when we fall.

I am believing with these women that their willingness to share their stories will not only complete the healing and deliverance process within their own lives, but also bring healing and deliverance to the many women who will read this book. I believe that chains will be broken, bondages will be loosed, and strongholds will be torn down and demolished.

I come against every stronghold of rejection, unworthiness, low self-esteem, depression, anger, rage, bitterness, unforgiveness, denial, lack. Break the shackles, and release to them a freedom and peace they have never experienced – peace in their minds, peace in their hearts and peace in their surroundings.

I break every word curse – intentional or unintentional – ever spoken or written over the lives of these women, let them be rendered impotent –

completely powerless. I cancel any attempt of the enemy to distort the purpose and intention of these writings and frustrate any agenda that is not of You.

I pray that each of these women finds the perfect will You have for each of their lives. Remove hindrances and stumbling blocks. Make the strategies clear. Gird them with the strength to remain tenacious and unyielding in the pursuit of the purpose You have called them to.

Cover them in their goings and comings, and we thank You and ask this in the mighty and indomitable name of Jesus. Amen.

Rebekah S. Hill

CHAPTER 1

Molestation, Money and Family

"Who knew this would be my life."

By: Kaleta Green

When you think you can trust people, they always disappoint you. The ones you love the most are the ones that hurt you the most. A beautiful baby girl was born on Dec 5th, 1971, and her name is Kaleta. By the time I was born, my parents had been together for ten years. My mother had three other children before she met my father. She had two daughters and a son. The oldest daughter, Estelle, died when she was only a few months old; then was my sister Erica and brother Bobby. My father had several kids from different women; I never got to meet them until I was older. Since I was the baby on both sides of the family, that means I should be very spoiled, right? That would be wrong! My childhood wasn't the best. In fact, it was very hard. I grew up in the projects of Roberts Park at 1510 Montserrado Place in Norfolk, Virginia. My life started to take shape at the age of two, and show me how it was going to be. I know you're like, "Wait. How at two? Can we talk for a minute?" At age two, I tried to kill my mom. Yes! At the age of two years old. Please, let me explain.

It was a typical day at home with the whole family, doing nothing, as usual. Mom was downstairs cooking pork chops, her and my dad's favorite meal; my siblings were each in their own bedrooms watching television. I was in the master bedroom with my dad. This day in particular, my dad was not paying me much attention because he was too preoccupied with combing his thick, black naturally wavy hair, that he was so fond of – attempting to lay it down just right with his trusty black tooth comb that he would always keep in his back trouser pocket.

My dad always had all his pocket change on the dresser along with his trusty black gun, which was right next to the television. On this day, as usual, he wasn't watching me like he should have been. So, me being curious, I took his gun off the dresser and walked to the top of the staircase and begin to yell for my mom to come to the bottom of the stairs.

I said, "Mommy come here!"

She proceeded to say, "What?"

"Momma come here!" I said again. My mom was ignoring me; she never came to the staircase, so I yelled again, "Mommy come here!"

My mom yelled back. "Bobby, see what that baby wants!"

I SUPPORT HER

When Bobby came to the stairs to see what I wanted, he panicked and yelled out for both my parents to come to the staircase. When my mom came to the bottom of the staircase, I proceeded to tell her, "I'm gone shoot" with my little two-year-old arms stretched out, while holding my dad's pistol that was squarely pointed at Momma's head with two hands.

Upon seeing me with that loaded gun pointed straight at her, my mom stood frozen at the bottom of the staircase. Too scared to move, too scared to do anything. Any sudden movement on her behalf might have startled me into accidently squeezing that trigger. All she could do was scream out for my dad. "Clarence, that baby got your gun!!!"

Then she spoke to me. She told me, "Kay-Kay, put the gun down!"

I repeated, "I'm gone shoot!"

As I cocked the gun back, a split-second right before I pulled the trigger, my brother and dad caught me in a simultaneous double bear hug and took the gun away from me. My mom told my dad to beat me; but all he did was take me in the room, told me not to do that again and popped me on the back of my hand. I should have known then that my life was going to be something to be reckoned with.

I never had a close relationship with my parents growing up. Some people have it bad living in a one parent household; I lived in a two-parent household for a while, and my childhood turned out to be just as bad with BOTH parents living under the same roof after the gun incident. My father was never around much. Once he and my mom separated, and my mom quickly settled into her new role of an aloof, absentee parent. Going in different directions and living separate lives, they were both too busy for little ol' me.

Back in the day, when my parents were still together, our house was known to have a lot of people around at any given time of day or night. My house was known as the "play church all day and party all night" house. You could catch all the hottest gospel groups at my house at any given moment backsliding and socializing. Everyone knew my mom; everyone hung out with her, and our door was always open. You could always rely on her for a meal, a glass of liquor, and a good time. Being very sociable and hospitable, my mom always kept the party going. She would always tell me to shut up and go upstairs when I would complain about the company she kept and the people she associated with.

There was no privacy, and my mother never set house rules and boundaries for those she was entertaining. I guess it was more important for her to make her guests feel comfortable and at home, than it was for me – her own daughter, the one who lived there – to feel comfortable. Since my mom didn't take my feelings into consideration, I felt uncomfortable most times.

To justify why the comfort of her guests was more important than her daughter's feelings, she would say, "He took care of you."

I would be like, "REALLY? By doing what?"

"How do you think you got those shoes or that outfit?" she would say.

Silly me, with my smart-alec mouth, would reply, "I thought you paid for my things?"

I SUPPORT HER

My mother had so many boyfriends who she made me call "Dad" – even though I had a dad and I knew who he was. My father was just not around. My mother would take on many lovers throughout the years and it used to really piss me off when she would want me to be nice to them because she would say, supposedly "He did that", "He did this" or "He brought you this." What a joke! They didn't buy it for me. They brought it because they knew that's what it would take to get with her. They could care less about me. Anything that I was "given" by her gentlemen friends was just the price of admission. Nothing more, nothing less.

The thing is – I can't fully blame her. She was doing what she felt needed to be done to get her and us kids by. The person I really blame is my dad, because he wasn't around at all. I felt as though he abandoned us. A parent should never take it out on the children. The children had nothing to do with the demise of my mom and dad's relationship. I felt this way strongly; especially more so with me because I was his biological child. So, ultimately, I was forced to call someone else Dad and I loved them all because they were always around.

As time went on, I found that my parents didn't split because they stopped loving each other. They split because they were both cheating and lying; according to my dad, he had finally had enough of the BS. But as they say, there's always two sides to a story. Not having that one steady, reliable man in the household, the streets were talking. There were certain rumors flying around and people were saying these bad and despicable things about my mom. They were embarrassing and I didn't want to believe them. But who am I to say anything about it? I was only a child. It wasn't like I was going to get into a verbal altercation with an ignorant adult who would repeat anything they heard about someone's mother in front of that child.

They would say slanderous things like: "Your mom is a "party girl" or "If your money was right, she was right." and it went on and on. The vicious lies, rumors, and gossip about my mom wouldn't stop. She was this, and she was that; as you can imagine, my mother was everything but a child of God. But that was hard to believe as a kid, mainly because we come from a very devout and religious family. You see, my mom growing up was one you would consider to be a "PK kid." (Preacher's Kid). I couldn't comprehend what the heck people were actually saying about her back then.

It's funny how the only person I was close to that had the courage to tell me about my parents was my aunt, Mary. At the time, she was my mom's best friend, and who also happens to be my dad's baby sister. She loved me and took care of me a lot of the time; and she would confide in me. Mostly by telling me why things were so messed up in my life and what really went down between my mom and dad. She always talked to me about my mom when I was growing up and there are some things that she shared with me, that I wished she had just kept to herself.

For the first time ever, I had my own bedroom. Since I was the baby, I always had to share with Bobby. We lived in a four-bedroom house and at this point, there was only three kids living with her. My sister Erica had gotten her own place on Chesapeake Blvd. in Norfolk. My brother, Bobby, would have been traveling with his band; he played the drums for a band that toured and so that kept him traveling a lot. So, it was my newborn baby brother, David and I.

I SUPPORT HER

My mom started putting me out at the age of 15

When my mom would put me out of the house, she would lie and tell people that I ran away, and that I was fast and disrespectful – none of which was true. But in this incident time, I was put out of the house for roughly around 6 months, for what this time only God knows. When my Mother saw fit to allow me back in the house, I wasn't allowed to go in my own bedroom. I had to dress in the downstairs half bath. I was relegated to sleep on the slate floors in the front room with one pillow, one sheet and one blanket like a dog. My mom wouldn't allow me to come upstairs. I had to ask permission to use her shower and if I went upstairs without permission to use her shower, I was accused of stealing from her.

I would be accused from stealing the simplest, basic household item -, her towels, wash clothes or sheets. Petty stuff, but you get the point. And to top all off – unless, I was taking a shower with *her* permission of course. I was to stay the rest of the time downstairs on that cold, dank, white slate floor. I wasn't allowed to go in *her* kitchen, if I got hungry, I couldn't even grab a snack, or watch *her* T.V. Eventually, out of spite, she eventually took *her* living room T.V. and *her* cordless kitchen telephone and locked those items in *her* bedroom so I wouldn't be tempted to use them. It was at these times, when she was playing all these mind games with me – being nasty for no reason and spiteful to me – that while sitting on *her* floor I would contemplate my next move.

My aunt was the only relative I had to help me when my mom put me out of the house for third time. Aunt Mary told me to leave my mom alone before I killed her or inflicted harm upon myself. By the age of 18 things had escalated so badly, that my mother's mistreatment had me on the brink of committing murder and suicide. Life was so bad I was having very lucid dreams and awake visions of killing her. I would envision her sitting in the dining room with other people, talking and laughing, and me just wrapping a rope around her neck and hanging her from the ceiling fan. Her company, whom she was entertaining, would just sit there watching me and not help her just as they have never helped me in life. I was having these visions, hallucinations day and night. At this point, I knew I needed help. I was seriously cracking up. To put it mildly, I felt as though if I didn't receive help soon, I was seriously going to kill her and then myself. At this point, I had already attempted suicide before, so I knew I was not scared to use a knife; I would use it on her before I did in myself. It had gotten so bad, that on this day, I was at my lowest. I was in the kitchen and I was adamant that today was as good a day as any to end it. I was on the verge of killing myself. I had already envisioned how I was going to do it as I tried to pick which knife was the sharpest. I wasn't going to attempt to slit my wrists again. It would take too long of a time to bleed out and I could be rescued before I do. I didn't want to be saved again.

Being found and saved was the only thing that prevented my last attempt. No, this time I wanted to kill myself by stabbing myself in the stomach with a steak knife. That way, if I was found bleeding and an attempt to save me was made the odds of resuscitation or revival would be slim because I discovered a gut puncture wound, especially one done by a large steak knife, would be almost fatal. I had the knife and I had the motive. I wanted to complete this, I really had a desire to see this through.

I had already written a goodbye letter inside my head because my mother didn't love me nor want me. I just wanted to be done with this life and maybe, just maybe, she would love me in death. No more stalling; I was tired. As I took the large steak knife and drew it back, as soon as I was about to do it, God must've made the home phone ring. The Most High had to be looking out for me that day because on the other end of the line was my favorite cousin, Paul. Paul always called or came around at the right times, it was like God sent him to be my guardian angel and he talked me down, gave me courage, inspired me and encouraged me to seek help. I cried hysterically over the phone and promised him that I would go speak to someone; I'd give this so-called life of mine yet another chance. At this point, I had nothing to lose but my life by my own hands so, I thought to myself "Why not?" That same day, I found myself on the #3 bus headed to TPI Tidewater Psychiatric Institute on Poplar Hall Drive in Norfolk, Virginia.

When I got there, I started talking to the intake worker and explaining to her what I was feeling and the vivid hallucinations I was having. I know I must've sounded like a nut job, because she immediately took me to the back, but I was telling my truth. There was no waiting or hesitation on her part. I figured I must have said all the key: "trigger words" to get someone with mental issues to be seen so suddenly. The doctor kept asking me repeatedly where my mom was and what did I do to her. Because of my vivid description of her death and my calm, nonchalant attitude I had while I was telling my story, along with the fact I just casually admitted I'm homicidal and suicidal and I just attempted to kill myself less than an hour ago. Had to have made that Psychiatric doctor freak out.

I SUPPORT HER

I can only imagine what was going through her mind. She probably thought she seen and heard everything until she and I crossed paths. I wasn't myself; I was lethargic and I was respectful but reckless by telling them so much of the things I was going to do and was in the process of doing to not only my Mom, but again to myself. I'm lucky I wasn't committed without my parents' consent. In a right frame of mind, I would have never said what I said to these Doctors or been so flippant and nonchalant about the whole thing. The scenario was surreal. It wasn't me and I felt as though I was having an out of body experience. I was looking down on me, hearing the words come out of me. I looked like me, but I know that it wasn't me. I was Zombified. These Doctors had to help, there was no choice I had given my Cousin Paul my word that I would give it one more try. If this had failed, then to many that was a clear sign for me knowing I had to do, what needed to be done. And, on an oft chance Paul happened to call back and catch me in the act sort of speak again. I would have said calmly: "Sorry Paul, you had your chance, love you, Bro" and I would have done it. As I am thinking these things.

I kept telling the Nurse and the Doctor what was going on and she was really trying to help but I was about to go to the 6th floor –Psych Ward. I was told to sign some papers to commit myself. Once that self-realization hit that they're trying to throw a strait jacket on me and contain me inside a rubber room. I remember "sobering up' quickly I mean I needed help but I knew I wasn't crazy or psychotic and I felt that were making me out to be something I'm not because of what I told. I was very conflicted on one hand I knew I needed help but not that type of help that they were trying to commit me to. So, when I got the chance to use the hospital's phone.

I SUPPORT HER

The first person I called was my Aunt Mary and I told her what was going on, I told her I was not myself and I knew I had made a mistake by being too open and too honest with Doctors who were just a little too eager to commit me. I just wanted some counseling not be a ward of Norfolk and be committed to the equivalent of a Hospital Jail. The first thing my Aunt told me to do was to call my Dad and I did, he told me he didn't want nothing to do with it. And that I need to figure it out on my own. That, was devastating. Here is your baby daughter looking for guidance and pleading out to you for emotional support from a Mental Institution's office phone and all he could say is: "naw, baby-girl cause I don't want to get involved" Wow!, that's all I could say just: "Wow!" Not making excuses for him, just giving you and explanation. To understand my Dad's way of thinking, you'd would have to know my Dad. My Dad is the type of person who never involves himself in one's personal problem whether it be his best friend's or his own Daughters' that just wasn't him. My Dad never wanted nor does he ever want to be involved with my life's problems and yes, he was very selfish in that way. I called my Aunt back and told her what my Dad had said, and man was my Aunt pissed and she was justified in her right to feel that way.

My Dad rejecting me like that as callously as he did, at the time and in that place. Could have triggered a major setback for me to the point, that the doctors would have had no choice but to commit me against my will for the sake of my wellbeing as well as for the safety of others. I shudder went I think about that moment and how the infliction and implication of my Dad's words could have gone south for me. Words have power people, remember that. Words have power. They can be used to lift you up or to break you down. My Aunt took it upon herself to call my Dad and gave him a piece of her mind. She told me not to sign anything and that my cousin Sandy was on her way to get me. Meanwhile they (meaning: The Psych Ward) had detained me in the back and had the police called to my mom's house to check up on her and see if she was actually dead or alive. I really did have those Doctors shook and they weren't taking any chances.

Precautions had to be taken, just in case my hallucinations I was telling them about was really a confession about me killing my mother. Can't say I blame them. I had more mental abuse by the hands of my Mom and I wished she was dead. This would make the second time before the age of 19 that I was on the fringes of killing my Mom. The 1st time was when I was 2 with the handgun remember? So, the police after seeing my Mom alive and well. They warn her about my visions to kill her. Now, my Mom knows everything. After my Psych evaluation, and I was officially released from the Institution's custody. The doctor warned me to stay away from my mom because she felt my Mom was a danger to my life & according to my Psychiatric evaluation, I was clearly exhibiting visible signs of someone having a nervous breakdown.

That Psychiatric evaluation is what lead me to stay at my Aunt's house for a few days in order to gather myself and to collect my thoughts, it was during this time that I finally mustered up the courage to call my mom and told her I needed to come home, partly because I knew I couldn't stay at my Aunt's house forever, I appreciate everything my Auntie has done for me, but two things were certain: 1. Ultimately I knew I wasn't her responsibility (not long term responsibility at least) and I didn't want to take advantage of her hospitality or to ever become a burden. I needed her and I didn't want any resentment. 2. I knew I needed to face my Mother sooner or later.

That was unavoidable and I couldn't hideout at my Auntie's house forever. The longer I thought about going back inside my Mother's house, the more I dreaded it. In the end, I couldn't bring myself to dial the home phone number because I knew there were going to be hell to pay and repercussions to be had. So, after much deliberate hemming and hawing on my part it was my Aunt who picked up the phone to call my Mom to be the "Ice breaker" and "Peace Maker" if you will. I'm not sure how my Mom responded because I could only hear my Aunt side of the phone conversation, but it went something like this & I am paraphrasing: "Sis, let that baby come home, she isn't sleeping on the streets, she'll be there tonight!" what my Aunt said and on the phone and how it went down totally differed. It would be a few more days later when I finally went back into that house and as you can expect my mother was there waiting for me. She was wide open and ready to pounce on me verbally. As soon as we locked eyes, she had something smart to say. Her only retribution would be Just to antagonize me and laugh in my face about what she was told by the policemen and what she knew or what she thought she knew was going on. She wasn't afraid of me or what I was capable of doing to her and she didn't care how I was feeling mentally, emotionally or spiritually.

All she cared about was having: "one up on me" it was this B.S. all over again. It was HER house; HER rules and it was HER time to shine and she was going to ride this wave of immature pettiness until the wheels fell off. My mom was Queen Petty and I can vividly remember her laughing and telling my business so loudly over the telephone because she wanted me to hear her talking smack about me in a way that was humiliating, degrading and at the same time she was provoking me and challenging me, daring me if you will to do something to her about it. My Mom was talking to Evelyn who is a family friend, about how I wanted her dead. And that I was going to die before her. All these theatrics over the phone was obviously for my benefit because she wanted me to hear her clowning me and as plain as the nose on my face. This act in itself clearly showed me, that she didn't love me.

Here I was an 18-year-old girl, who obviously was in pain, crying for help and attention and like my Dad before her all I got was the opposite. All I wanted was for my Mom to love me and to except me for who I was. At this point I was so flustered & exasperated, All I could blurt out somewhat coherently is: "What is wrong with me, why don't you love me, what's wrong with me. WHAT IS IT?! WHY DON'T YOU LOVE ME?!!!" My Mom just stood with the cordless phone in her right hand pressed firmly against her right breast trying to muffle any words that I might say, so that they wouldn't get within earshot of Evelyn who I could only imagine was trying to eavesdrop every syllable on the other end. Because my Mom had a way of controlling the narrative and manipulating the way people felt and thought about her. She was never the "bad guy" she painted the picture that she was and is a good Mom and it was 'I' who had the problem. It was I they wouldn't conform, or go along with the plan.

I was the rebellious daughter who needed structure and discipline, My Mother would never admit the role she played in my life. The hurt, sorrow and anguished she caused, not only to me but also to my father and my siblings. And so there she stood expressionless, muffling the phone and after all that emotion just poured out of 18-year-old me. All my Mom could say to me was: "Get Out Of My Face!" My dear Aunt Mary passed away a few years ago she was my heart, my advocate, my support system and my protector and now that she is gone, I have no one that truly loves me, I'm all alone now...... Don't get me wrong, for the most part, if nothing else, I had my siblings and I'm sure by this time you're wondering where were my brother and sister at during this tremulous period in my young life, right?

Well, at this point, as I've stated previously my brother Bobby who is a phenomenal Drummer was almost always gone. He was out making a name for himself & touring the world over with his band which kept him away from home months on end, and then there was my older sister & my new born baby brother David. I being the baby in the family with older siblings, the younger ones always tend to cling to the older ones that shows you the most attention. For me, that person was my sister Erica.

No one was more beautiful as my big sister. She had a beautiful light skin complexion and beautiful hair, that good type of hair you just throw water on and her mane just waves up. Funny, I know, but you know that type. I used to look up to my sister she was everything I wanted to be, so I thought. She was my 2nd mom she took care of me and my brother 90% of the time. She was the one who took me to school & I looked to her to chaperone whenever my class went on field trips & when I got pregnant at the tender age of 13 (another story, that I will explain later in the book.) Erica was the one that took me to the hospital to find out if I really was indeed pregnant.

Erica would take us shopping, buy us clothes, etc. etc. I think by now, some of you are starting to get the picture. I would try to imitate everything she's did, you know in that little sister way, that was probably really irritating to my big sis. I don't know, and if I was, my sister had

I SUPPORT HER

such an air of coolness about her, that she'd never show it if I was, I may be young, but I wasn't naïve. I am having a good time being around, hanging and emulating my big sister, but at the same time I am worried and a little concerned about where was she getting the money from to buy all these things? Even as a young girl I was a worrier by nature and consciously aware to a fault and the last thing I would ever want to do is to take advantage of my sister's generosity. But like the cat, curiosity has gotten the better of me & in the back of my mind, I am wondering how she could afford dresses like this and to dress the way she was dressing, back in those days, my sister was always one of the flyest dressers in Hampton Roads, hands down. So, exactly where was this money coming from? I needed to find out. She wasn't getting it from our Mama that's for sure especially if my Mom knew Erica was going to spend some of it on me. No, way. She wasn't working or had a job as far as I knew. And she or rather I should say "we" frequently shopped at JCPenney.

At that time shopping at JCPenney was a big deal. For all intents and purposes considered a very affluent and expensive white people store. You weren't going into JCPenney to browse. Those white folk's salespeople would chase off young black kids quickly if they felt you didn't have a dime to spend. At this particular point and time, Erica was shopping at this establishment quite frequently, so the sales people took to Erica because they knew home girl was coming in to spend money, not to take up space being a "window shopper" in particular I can remember this one time when she took me to get my ears pierced and that was amazing because I wanted to be just like her, My sister had her ears pierced so naturally I wanted mines done also.

I SUPPORT HER

It was simple stuff like that, that would bring me joy in an otherwise bleak and depressing life I lived in. I couldn't get enough, anything Erica had that she valued I wanted. But, again. Where was this money coming from at the age of 13? Yes, I'd be the first to admit. Erica did have a few boyfriends, but nothing major, but that's to be expected she was gorgeous, popular, could cook (even at the age of 13 the girl was putting whole meals together.) has a great singing voice (she sings in a choir and was known in our church community for holding her own during church solo's.) and she could lay some hair. There was no need for me to go to a salon. In fact, her hairstyling skills were so great I often mimicked a lot of her styles on my daughter and god kids. I used to think I have to be like my big sis. My sister had this one Man (and that's not a metaphor for boyfriend). I do mean Man. As in a Grown Ass Man in her life that did a lot of stuff for her. I being younger just never knew who he was to her, because he was so much older than her. I'm talking obscenely older. As in 40yrs her senior older.

This Man used to take her shopping and give her money and pay her bills. Whatever she wanted, she had it. I HATED THIS MAN with a passion, I didn't know why but I did. Maybe it was a tinge of jealousy, not because he was giving her things, that wasn't it. Erica was generous to a fault and would share or even give me anything she got. The jealousy was more from him taking up her time, valuable quality time that I thought could have been better spent with me. Being with my sister was very important to me, even more so as I got older. Being with her I knew I was safe, and just as importantly I knew I could count on her.

To be honest at first, I thought Mr. Diggs was her Godfather but came to find out he played a bigger role in Erica's life. You see my family has harbored a long-kept secret. A BIG SECRET. So, Secret. That only my grandmother knew…. When you're young you'd think your Mom is your savior but when you find out the truth, that you're just an object in the way of her happiness, primarily because she was no longer with my Father, then, I was no longer of any use to her. It was then at a very young age, before I even heard the saying or knew what it meant "you have to sink or swim'. See my mom has never told me she loves me. Please allow me to say it again: MY MOTHER HAS NEVER TOLD ME SHE LOVED ME. And I guess she never will. But she'd have zero problems with telling her baby girl she wished I was never born. For the life of me, I don't know where all my Mom's hatred towards her own daughter stems from, but I do know this for sure. It could only be one of two things. Or maybe for her it's both: either because I look just like my Dad or maybe it's because my dad had enough sense to get away from her ass early in their volatile, ups and down relationship. And seeing me all the time was somehow a trigger for her or a reminder of how she let a "good one" like my Daddy get away.

My Daddy is a Man who kept A good job, worked hard and went to work every day, came home to his family, put food on the table, paid bills and wasn't for no foolishness. I know my Mom missed that and in turn missed him. Cause if my Dad wasn't anything, he was stability, calmness, structure and if you remember anything about the gun incident when I was only 2 a sense of safeness. That is why, I truly believe just the look of me or the sound of my voice would make my Mom go from 0 to 100 real quick. She was bitter and just always mad at me for something. All I could do was just throw up my hands in exasperation and just mutter to myself: "Lord what did I do wrong this time?"

I SUPPORT HER

A child shouldn't feel like they're mother hates everything about them. But growing up in my mother's house, that's how she'd made me feel. And I am quite sure she knew that was the type of vibe and energy she was giving off to me because she has never gone out of her way to make me feel anything different. Further cementing the fact that my feeling some type of way, about how my Mom feels about me at such a young, impressionable and awkward age. Wasn't about me just being in my feelings. It felt like her truth. I hate to sound like a broken record. So, I will say it again for the last time: All I wanted was for her to love me that's it. A hug, A kiss or to tell me she loved me and I was a good girl but that has NEVER happened and if I was a gambling woman. I would probably bet on it. It never will, not in this life. My mother is still alive, to make amends, to right the wrongs and to make all the pain, agony and anguish go away...so who knows? Maybe, just maybe - one day GOD will answer my prayers and grant me that one wish. I'm more inclined to believe all this is just WISHFUL thinking on a FOOLISH WOMAN's part. But I'm allowed to DREAM am I not?

Now, there were many occasions when my Mom would go visiting my uncle who lived out of town or be gone for any extended length of time. When my mom would leave, I would get physically ill but by her sheer absence alone and you'd think I would be jumping for joy and elated by her being away whether it'd be for a few days or even a few hours. But I wouldn't get myself emotionally sick and heart stricken (as if I just lost my puppy.) and I used to cry myself to sleep. Why? I don't know why...probably because as bad as she used to treat me and as bad as she made me feel. At the end of the day I was just a little girl who wanted her Mommy.

I know this may be foreign to some of y'all. But I loved my Mom then and I still do to this day. I never stopped loving my Mom. No matter how abusive, estranged, coldhearted, conniving, manipulative and delusional and sociopathic signs she might exhibit, she's still my Mother and you only get one. I didn't know anything else. So, even at a young age I knew my Mom was different from other Moms. I couldn't tell you how, but I knew she was "off" and that I was just going to have to make the best of a very bad situation. Even if I had to beg literally and figuratively for some type of love and affection from her. But alas, no matter what I did. I just wasn't on her radar. My family on my Mother's side. Came from some of the most incredible people in my life, my Grandparents. My Grandparents they were the 2 people that kept the Moore family together. Erica was very close to our Grandma. In fact, she was more of a mom to Erica than our mother, but I didn't understand the bond of their relationship. I used to be jealous because I didn't have that bond with my Grandmother, only with my Granddaddy. See we come from a very religious family, my Granddad was a Bishop and Grandma was a true Elder not like these false prophets who are good at just playing church like I have seen these days.

All of my family are musicians, singers and some have heard the calling to become ministers. Collectively we can play just about every musical instrument. Truthfully, I may be the only one who wasn't musically inclined when it came to playing music. But I could sing and preach so I didn't fall too far from the family talent tree. I just wasn't blessed with nimble fingers for the guitar, keyboard or drums. The Moore Clan as my family would become to be known as should have been famous right now for our naturally gifted talents. if we didn't carry the burden of the secrets that we do and the petty jealousies we harbored

I SUPPORT HER

of each other and the ones we still have we could have left 757 and been a household name like the "Wynans" or the "Isleys". Maybe not as big, but big enough to have been internationally recognized.

My Grandparents were pioneers of the gospel and Erica was in church more often than not. From sunup to sundown and where was I when I was allowed to go? With her, and it was a blast. It was no secret. I loved church, I wanted to go to church. No one had to force us to go and unlike some of today's kids. I didn't mind being in church sometimes 12, 13 or 14hrs. The church was my sanctuary. The shouting, the praising, the music, the preaching it was amazing! And oh yeah, the boys. The only thing I didn't like about her church was my grandmother used to separate the church by gender. The boys were seated on the left and all the girls were seated in the pews to the right. It was during these times when I used to think: why JESUS why?

I used to think my Grandmother was mean spirited and she didn't like nor love me because she barely talked to me unlike how she would open up and confide in my sister. When she wasn't performing her churchly duties. All her free time was freely spent with Erica, I didn't know it back then, but now I know why and part of me wishes that I didn't know at all. Before my Granny died, she told my sister's ex-boyfriend Clinton to look out for her baby Erica and to make sure she is ok. I am of the belief that the hardest thing my Grandma ever had to do was leaving my sister here alone to fend for herself. The thing is when you are growing up all you want is to be protected and loved, but some people that is the hardest thing to give.

Growing up Erica started dating a man named: Wilson Paul who was only 19 yrs. old at the time. He, too, like Mr. Diggs, was very old to me, with a head full of grey hair and all. He knew my Mom intimately. Actually, they used to date back in the day if you can believe that. My sisters' life and mine intertwine so much at times it's scary. I didn't know how hard her life was compared to mine, probably because I was enraptured in my own drama. But she handled it against all odds and you'd never know what was going on in her life or inside her head because of her strong exterior. Erica, would never show openly, outward signs of distress. It just wasn't who she was. I was always the black sheep in the family, and, well, Erica was: "the Special One" and I believe the only reason she was "so special" was because Erica was the type to always do whatever our mom told her to do. I don't believe my sister loved or liked these old ass men. Hell. I'm grown now, and I don't want no old geezer talking to me or touching me at all. I trusted Wilson Paul. I genuinely, really liked him until the one day he gave me a reason not to. Let me tell you the story.

To give you some context. I will start from the beginning... One day my sister went out of town to New York to visit my Uncle. With Wilson her BF hanging around the house to help my Mom and Brother paint his room that afternoon. Fast forward to that night. Roughly around 9PM or so. I fell asleep in Erica's room which was right next door to my brother Bobby's. The bedrooms in our house are close. So, close in fact that the only thing that separated my sister's room and Bobby's was a shared outer wall. So, for the life of me. I cannot understand what this Man was thinking. When I tell you that Wilson took it upon himself to come into the room where I was. For what? Only GOD knows. My Mom always trusted people around her daughters no matter who they were or for how short of a time she's known them.

I SUPPORT HER

While I was asleep with the bedroom lights on, Wilson took his fingers through a hole in my pajamas and proceeded to finger my vagina. I was so shocked and startled. I practically jumped off the bed and was horrified to discover that it was Paul Wilson! My Mother's friend, my sister's boyfriend as well as a friend of mine or so I thought he was a friend up until this moment. I couldn't understand why he was violating me like this. I couldn't believe what had just happened, I couldn't believe that it was in my own house, I couldn't believe he had the audacity to even try something like that with my Mother and Brother literally in the other room painting right next door, in Erica's room no less. with the lights on. Just so many thoughts running through my head at once. This felt like a bad dream, one I was hoping to wake up from. This couldn't be reality; it just couldn't be. I trusted him until he gave me a reason not to. After I jumped up, he tried to quiet me down, he told me to go back to sleep and left a $1 dollar bill on the yellow and green plastic kitchen chair which stood next to the bed.

After he did the dirty deed he was leaving like a thief in the night. I then heard Paul mention he was going to church with us. I couldn't scream. I just played like I was asleep. After the house got quiet, I got up lookin around. Once I realized, Wilson left. The first thing I did was run to my mom's room where my Mother and her boyfriend were in the bed. When I told my mom, what happened I expected my Mother to be enraged, angry, and upset and Mommy's gonna' protect you. I got none of that. I thought We are marching down to that police station tomorrow and put charges on Wilson's ass!" Except that is not reality, because that is not what I got.

I SUPPORT HER

Truthfully, during this upsetting moment when my Mother had the chance to rescue me. This is what I got: Knock! Knock! (Me knocking on her bedroom door) My Mom responds with: "YES open the door?!" I said: Mom! Wilson touched me! "What do you mean? "He touched me down there!" "You're lying!" My Mother retorted back. "No! I'm not" I said. "She said you're lying, go back to bed". This whole scenario was unreal, this couldn't be my life. I just got molested in this place I call home by a family friend and now I. the innocent victim in all of this. Is being accused of lying. I just stood there and I gave both my Mother and her brother who just stood beside her looking stupid, not saying anything. it felt as though I just stood there staring at them in disbelief for an eternity without a single word being spoken by anyone until I decided it would be in my best interest to just turn around and walk away. If I didn't know it before then, I knew now how my Mother truly felt about me. Did I need any more proof? Even at a young age, I had an awareness about me that most kids either don't possess or it doesn't develop until adulthood. I had the awareness to know back then that no one would believe me and that I was on my own at the tender age of 8.

Next morning no talk about what I said last night I was the victim and my mom didn't believe me. Overwhelmingly, women who find themselves at the forefront of an uncompromising situation, who are then led to believe that somehow this is their fault instead of placing blame on the aggressor. It is always the victim's fault for "allowing" herself to be in that situation. One who wouldn't have anything to gain by lying about something as personal and embarrassing as child sexual assault? To even suggest that I falsely accused someone of something like that, would show that I was well versed & schooled in the art of manipulation, seduction, coercion and extortion.

You'd have to be real sick individual to believe that somehow an undeveloped 8 year girl knew the powers of her womanly charms (and I use that term loosely) and somehow seduced or made this grown- ass man believe I wanted, enticed or in some way implied I wanted him in a sexual manner. How can anyone with a half a brain sexualize a young girl like that? The following day, Sunday Morning. Nothing changed for me sitting in the kitchen getting my hair down. It was business as usual in my house and we had to get ready for church. It was as if the biggest bombshell I dropped late last night about a Man putting his fingers inside me never happened, my Mom carried on. Getting herself prepared for Sunday service as if I never said anything. I was scared, I was ashamed and above all else I was hurt and disappointed.

How did this happen to me and where was my Daddy? I didn't want to go. I didn't want to get in Wilson Paul's car. I can still remember when Wilson pulled up to the house that day to pick us up. With all of my family members running to the freaking car, like it's the Batmobile or something. But I wasn't going, Hell NO! I'm not going. I had my mind made up. I could hear my Mother from the car asking Bobby where is Kay, I could distinctly hear my mother repeatedly calling my name: "Kay- Kay, where is Kay-Kay?" I wasn't listening and I wasn't answering. I was going to ignore her, after a while, she sent my brother Bobby in after me. "Where is she?" I knew she saw my head peeping down on her from an upstairs bedroom window.

Even, so, It didn't matter. I stood strong in my standoff. At only 8 I was as stubborn as ever. And in my stubborn defiance I determined that NO ONE will ever see my body again. I'm no liar. He did this. Here comes Bobby to relay our Mother's message to tell me what I already know. "To come on there, waiting on me." I told him with as much courage as an 8yr. old could muster: "I'M NOT GOING!" but being a child, I had to go, who was going to stay home with me? The answer is: No one unfortunately. You see my brother Bobby was the churches Drummer and my Mom was the churches Organist and regardless of past circumstances and transgressions. I had to sing at church as usual. If I couldn't tell my Mom, who could I tell? She was supposed to protect me, what happened!? Sunday service has always been my highlight, this is the place and the day I looked forward to the most solely because I'd get to show off my vocals, but today I'm saddened by this burden I have to carry around with me and I'm not in the mood. Do you know what it's like for your molester to pick you and your family up for church while driving you to the house of the Lord as if everything is cool? I pray you'd never know that feeling.

With my Mom chatting him up in the front passenger seat as he's driving and I can literally feel the tension in the air. Because everyone in that car (Me, My Mother, Bobby and my Mother's Boyfriend.) knew on that Sunday drive what he had done and I know that I was no liar, but if you let my brother tell it I make up stories. But here is everyone making stupid small talk as if it's water under the bridge or as if what he did was just some sort of minor inconvenience. A "My bad, I shouldn't have done that to your underage daughter" situation. I'm sitting in the backseat of this Man's car trying my best to drown out this small talk everyone seems to be engaged in & the voice inside my head is screaming out: "Mom! Are you seriously not going to mention what I said to you last night?" aren't you going to ask me if I am alright?" "Wow! Nothing?" "NOPE!" nothing.

I hated my Mom after the fact and my family as well. Mainly for not believing me. Again, why would I lie? No one came to my aid, no one came to my defense. A few days later Erica came home from her trip. I was very conflicted. On one hand I was so happy to see her. I must've been grinning from ear to ear like a Cheshire cat and on the other hand I dreaded seeing her because I knew I needed to tell her about "the incident" and I knew she wouldn't take the news well. If this is not a family cover-up, I don't know what is, but I was told not to tell her what happened. That I was a liar and to never speak of this again, but I knew I needed her to know the man that she is dating touched me. I was definitely at a crossroads because I had no ill intentions of hurting my sister when I can clearly see she's happy.

Erica started to really fall for this guy and I wanted desperately to tell her about this, before she married this man. It just so happened that a few years later Erica walked in on us (my Mom, myself and Bobby) talking about it one day at my mom's new house and she overheard our mom say "don't tell her" Erica responded with: "don't tell me what" and when Erica said that we all jumped a little because our scandalous family secret, had just been busted and that was the day. Erica would finally know the truth and I could offload this burden of carrying it around and keeping it a dirty secret off of my chest.

Doing so felt as though a heavy weight had just been lifted and I told her EVERYTHING. I told her how Wilson put his fingers in my vagina in your bed and paid me a $1 afterwards to do so. She poignantly asked my mom: "why didn't you tell me? Why did you keep that to yourself? My Mom and Bobby weakly replied: "because you know she (referring to me) lies! And make up stories!" I explained to Erica how I tried to tell Mom when it happened, but that she was very dismissive of me and told me to go back to bed. Erica as you can imagine left the house very upset and confused, but in hindsight. I'd guess the ordeal I went through wasn't enough to be a relationship deal breaker for her. Because, guess what? She married my Molester anyway.

Now, ain't that a blip! Circling back to my Mom. My mom was and still is to this day a great manipulator. She could turn any and every one against me faster than FEDEX'S One day deliveries and she could tell you a story about me that you'd swear on the gospel was the GOD's honest truth. That's how good my Mom was. When it came to how people felt about me. My Mother always controlled the narrative and her expert timing, because she would always get out ahead of me to tell her tall tale to anyone listening before I had a chance to tell my side. So, by the time I did get a chance to speak up for myself.

Negative opinions were already formed of me. Battle lines were drawn prematurely and sides were taken especially with family (which was usually my Mother' side) and for as long as I can remember that is how life for me always been. It still pains me to this day. To have my sister find out in the way that she'd done. I didn't want for it to go down like that. I wanted to be the one to address the issue with her one on one. In private. I knew she was hurt and devastated, and the last thing I wanted to do was to hurt my sister, but she married him anyway, and I guess she was happy at least I liked to think that she was happy. Here I was victimized at 8, ridiculed, ignored and chastised about it and through all of that. Despite everything else, I was still worried about my sister's feelings. She and Wilson Paul would marry a year after I told her of the incident and coincidentally, I would never forgive my family for not believing me. Erica and I were still close and my being around didn't stop Wilson.

I remember coming over to their place to visit off Diamond Springs Road and on this particular day, we had just come in the house from the beach and fishing. I had on a black one-piece bathing suit that my cousin Janice had given me. it was so cute. It was all black with a little whole over the top with a knot and I had on some blue jean shorts. Wilson kept urging me to take off my jean shorts and I was like NOPE NEVER and ran off the pier! While he was asking this, Erica was running around somewhere talking to my mom and my brother Bobby's dad. I'm still uncertain how my sister and I got separated and I ended up alone on the Pier with him.

I kept that incident to myself and I didn't say anything. Later that day Erica wanted me to come back with her to her house. She and I was having so much fun together she didn't want the day to end. Of course, I was like Cool I love being with my sister no matter the circumstances or who she was married to. No one was going to stop me from hanging with her and when I'm with her I do tend to feel safe. Late that night when we were all in our bedrooms and I could distinctly hear my sister and Wilson having sex. So, I felt ok. I'm safe. I felt as though with my Sister having just given her Husband what he wanted his desire to come messing with me would have been sedated. Nope, once again I was wrong. Right after he was finished with her, he made a beeline for my room and started rummaging through my bags, found a pair of my used panties, put them to his nostrils and started inhaling my scent. As this was done, right in

I SUPPORT HER

front of me, while I laid motionless in bed and pretending to be sleeping. WTF is wrong with this guy.

He was a depraved pedophile in the worst way, a monster who would take extreme risks just to get a sniff of me. The only difference between this day and a year in a half ago is: MY MOLESTER WAS NOW MY BROTHER IN LAW. Let's let that one sink in for a minute. And what's really crazy is that when I turned 13. Whenever he felt like he could get away with it he'd make these very inappropriate sexual comments. Like, one time I could clearly remember him saying to me: "If you're going to have sex, don't just lay there - get up and go pee" Like really? I'm 13 dude, get the hell away from me sicko. Wilson also taught me to know my truth and never let my truth stop me from being who I'm destined to be. You know being the baby you never know what your other siblings are going through and what your mom has done to them. See our secrets are meant to destroy us to break us down.

My sister thought my mom loved her but she didn't know at birth she was going to be a financial come up for our mom. I never thought this would be my life yet alone my family. Why, how can you do what you have done. Now I understand why it was ok for Wilson to touch me that's why it was ok for him to still come around. all I wanted was to be loved by you but that was too hard to do. A child is to be loved and a child is not supposed to be produced for profit. They need your protection; they need to be nourished and loved. I was told I was a product of love from my dad, but I guess she fell out of love with him and immediately stopped caring for me. I was not to be touched for your financial pleasures.

Instead you hated me that much to allow someone to use and abuse me and my sister. the most sacred thing I have is my jane as my grandmother called it. You let it happen not once but a few times and not just to me. WHY didn't you love me? WHAT did I do to you? The thing is when I threatened to shoot you at age 2 in my mind, I should have, sad to say but that's how I felt growing up, maybe Erica's life would have been much happier. I remember when I got that phone call and to this day when I think about it, I cringe. you still don't know that we know what you did. you think we're just distant for nothing you think she has no right to be mad at you., you think because he's dead your secret is safe no its not, we know about everything. We know it was for $20.00, is that all WE ARE worth to you?

A lifetime of pain is worth a half a tank of gas to you. All we want to know is WHY and that you're sorry but we'll or shall I say she will never get that from you. Having felt like she had to jump out of windows to get away from certain people why? Why did you hate us why did you hate her? what did she do to make you feel like she was worthless less than beneath your feet WHAT WAS IT ? just know IN 2001 I got that call from her asking me did I know what you did I had to console her I had to let her know I loved her and I was here for her. On that day I wished you were dead. Just because you go to church doesn't stop the pain and the shame you made us feel.

You must understand when you allow your ex-boyfriend that is now in his 40's to date your teenage daughter something has to be wrong with you. Now I see why grandma held on so tightly to Erica because she knew what was going on and so do a lot more people but all of your secrets are safe with them... unlike my dad because he knows who you were but he isn't going to say anything why because he doesn't want to get involved. All we want right now is for you to go to my sister and say you're sorry and Admit your wrong so we can heal from this we all need that as well as you. Yes, we both know about the 20.00 now I get it. Let me explain: Mr. Diggs asked for her to come see him when he was ill, and she went but what she didn't know why? Why did he want to see her after all these years? This was the biggest secret and disappointment a mother could do to a child.

Let's go back. I got married to a wonderful man named Bryan Myers. He was 7 yrs. younger than me he but you can call him my savior he really knew how a man supposed to treat a woman and he loved me unconditionally. One day I got that call from my sis she was upset crying uncontrollably screaming "Did you know? "she screamed. I thought my mom had died because she was still close to her, but the words that came out of her mouth were unbelievable to this day. "she asked did you know "calm down I said know what"? "what momma did, I repeated "what?" calm down what did she do by this time were both married, and.

Erica said "I went to see him" ok and" he was apologizing Erica said. "for what" I said? she then started to say I always wondered "WHY ME?" "I always why he never left me alone why me kay why me "she cried to the point I started crying, the pain you feel after you hear someone has died. I'm going to leave you with this forgiveness is not for the person that wronged you, it's for you to be released to be free, to stop the shame that we may feel. Love the person that hates you. It will make them think twice about hurting you, maybe it won't but GOD will allow you to heal in his time not in yours. see I don't look at my parents in a bad light anymore because I see it like this, they gave me what they could and what they couldn't I just didn't get.

Even when I was sleeping outside, I still forgave my mom and dad and I still loved them. Being in abusive relationships and telling my mother and she did nothing. I still loved her and forgave her. See I was always looking for her to say great job for her to love and to just accept me but I was not worthy enough for that to happen but I know I am because god told me so. You can't let your past dictate your future. I used to tell people my mom wasn't my mom she was a friend of my mom and my mother was away in the military. I was out of place. I had in my mind what my mom and dad should be, they were the total opposite. I feel I was born to parents that couldn't deal with the fact I was greater than what they expected me to be. they didn't have enough love to give me when I came along; they only had a few pints of love left and that was not enough to sustain my life.

I'm going to say this, forgiveness is not giving up the hope that the past could be any different. It's for you to be free so God can move in your life. You think forgiving means accepting what has happened to you but it's accepting that it HAS happened to you. NOT that it was ok but that it's in your past. I don't hold grudges because it is a killer. Don't hold on to what people have done to you forgive them. FORGIVENESS IS A GIFT YOU GIVE YOURSELF. FORGIVE.

CHAPTER 2

A Mother's Ordeal

"Dealing with Breast Cancer…My Own Way,"!

By: Gloria Jean Eason

I can remember it like it was yesterday, my best friend, my mother succumbed to her horrific but courageous battle with breast cancer! I felt lost, there was a huge hole in my heart, and I desperately wanted my mother back, but that was selfish, I knew she was no longer suffering. Thinking back saddens me, I reminisce about how vibrant and full of life my mother was, and how tragically her life was cut short by this horrible disease, breast cancer. Just saying it makes all the feelings flood back and I think why can't this be prevented. Why with all our great discoveries, a cure for breast cancer is not available! The year after the attacks of 9/11, I received a temporary job assignment in San Diego. My mother was distraught that I had to get on a plane and fly for five hours.

I understood, I was scared too, truth be told many people were suddenly afraid to fly after the attacks of 9/11. I had never flown before, I always traveled by car; however, the job was not allowing that, so I had no choice. My mother was so scared for me, she said "if you see any of those people get off the damn plane". I knew what she meant, but my mother like many people still thought all people from Arab countries were terrorists. I never told my mother this, but low and behold when I got on the plane that day with my coworker, one of "those" people was in the seat right beside me. We were all seated in the very last aisle in the back of the plane for the first flight to Dallas before continuing on to San Diego. I was so nervous, so I suddenly wanted to do as my mother instructed and get the hell off the damn plane. It was already too late; the door was closed and the plane was already speeding down the runway. My nerves were so bad, I was shaking and holding on to my coworker; I felt as if I was shaking just as much as the plane was. I could hear was my mother's voice play over and over again in my head "get off the plane, get off the damn plane!". When we arrived in Dallas, I was so happy, even though it was just a layover. I immediately called my mother and told her that I had already made it safely to California so she wouldn't worry about me so much. It was important for me to ease my mother's mind about my safety. I did not want my kind and loving mother, with the beautiful spirit that made everyone love and admire her, spending her day in a heap of nerves worried about my safety, when it was out of our hands. We made it to California and I knew I had spared my mother worry and that gave me peace. No matter how old you get, for most of us, your mother is always your rock.

Thinking back, I was in my hotel room in San Diego, getting ready for work and my sister called. My sister wanted to tell me my mother was not her usual self; she did not think my mother felt good but my mother wasn't saying anything about it. When I asked my sister what was different, she said my mother was sleeping excessively and never wanted to get out of the house and go anywhere. Thinking about that, I thought that was very unusual for my mother. My mother absolutely loved to shop, go to bingo and visit one of her sisters who lived only minutes away on the same road. My siblings and I had a four-way group phone conversation, discussing what we thought could possibly be wrong with our mother. My first thoughts where she was just tired from all the housework and cooking, she does every day and the added burden of looking after my two children while I was away. My mind never went to thinking the worst, I thought my mother would tell me if she was thought she was really sick. Nothing was changing though, I just kept worrying and thinking about her more and more every day. I called her every single day and she seemed fine, but I couldn't tell physically because I couldn't see her, so in my mind my mother was good. The phone calls went from calling her twice a day morning and night, to calling her four to five times a day because I just wanted to hear her voice and know she was alright. My mother was wonderful and always made me feel good about leaving my kids for a work assignment. I can still hear her say to me, "Don't worry about them crazy kids of yours. Me and your dad got them. If they get to be too much, I am going to beat their ass back into shape." I needed this peace of mind my mother provided so I would not worry about my young children and she knew it, and provided me with it every day.

    My mother seemed to be fine and that was my thought; no one, not even my sister, could make me think anything different. While I was in California, if I called my mother and she didn't answer, I would go off into a panic mode. In the back of my mind something still seemed wrong, maybe intuition, a gut feeling you get when you can't pinpoint a problem. At times I was like a lunatic, calling her a hundred times, I didn't care I needed to hear her voice just to know she was still doing fine. When she finally would call back a sigh of relief would come over me and she would say to me "Why the hell you keep calling me if I don't answer you know I must be sleep or cooking." My mother truly was a hilarious and witty woman with colorful metaphors that would make me laugh so hard and ease my mind being far away and all alone. Still, with all the phone calls and the words to try and put me at ease, I could not forget the phone call with my siblings and that nagging feeling I could not shake that something was not right. One late afternoon, my phone rang, and it was my mother. She said to me that she was just not feeling good.

I kept asking what was wrong and she would say to me, "It's only my blood pressure" or "It's only a slight headache."

I said to her, "Please, Mom. Go to the doctor."

"You know me and your dad don't have any health insurance, so we would have to pay out of pocket," she replied.

I said, "Mom, come on; you are taking care of my babies. I will wire you some money to go to the doctor and get your medicine."

My mother was the type that would not take money from her children, end of story! She was unemployed because of an accident; she had gotten some chemicals in her eyes, which caused her to develop high blood pressure. Even though this was a financial burden, my mom was still happy, loving and very courageous with no job and no health insurance. My mother was never angry, she loved us all the same. When it came to her grandkids, she loved them the most. In her opinion, they didn't ask to be born and you as a parent were going to take care of them until they were old enough to take care of themselves. I remember when I first start working at the job, I had my daughter and then her brother four years later. My mother would watch the kids for me and my cousin. Since she wouldn't take money for nothing, this was our way around it. That was how we made sure she had some money in her pocket to get her medicine and pay some of her doctor's bills. We didn't have to pay her for watching the babies, we just knew it was the only way to give her money to help her to get her medicine. In early May of 2002, I was scheduled to leave to come back home from California, our assignment was almost completed. I was so ready to leave California, I was desperately homesick for my family, and hated the work in California. In Norfolk, the company knew that I was an extremely dedicated and hardworking supervisor; in California they did not show me the same respect I was deserving of.

We arrived at the airport around ten o'clock Monday morning Our flight was scheduled to leave around noon, and I was very excited and nervous. I called my mother and I told her I was at the airport waiting for my flight to leave to come home, she was so happy to hear that. Once again, my mother was a nervous wreck. In hindsight, maybe I should have just called her once I was home and surprised her so she would not have worried. I remember calling her back and telling her that we had a layover and I was not going to be home at the time that I originally told her. Her mind went right to panic mode and she said, "Why the hell not? Is something wrong with the plane or is something wrong with you?" My mom was such a trip, she knew I could not lie to her at all, so I explained nothing was wrong – sometimes there were flight delays and layovers. Still not satisfied, she just told me to get home as soon as I could; "I need you to pick these kids up. They are getting on my nerves," she said. I never questioned why she said they were getting on her nerves. She had her own reasons and she was doing something great for me by watching them while

I was away. Reflecting back, I believe my mother was holding on in part for me, because by this time, she was already very ill but still not admitting it for my sake.

I arrived home about 10:30 that night. I was exhausted, but I had to go get my children and see my mother after 5 months away. When I got to my mother's house, I went in and I saw my mother laying on the couch. TD Jakes was preaching on the TV and I remember him saying to God be the glory, all things are possible through Christ; I remember saying amen. My mother was quite surprised to see me home. She got up and we hugged like we had never hugged before, so happy to finally be together. My mother was such a beautiful woman, she was barely past 60 but looked much younger. She had dark skin and her hair was naturally curly. I think being both black and of Cherokee Indian ancestry, gave her a special beauty. My mother had shown me pictures of my great-grandmother, and I could see how beautiful she was. My great-grandmother's hair hung all the way down her back she appeared to be only five-foot-tall at best and was absolutely stunning. I now understood where my mother got her beauty from. My mother seemed to never age, not a wrinkle to be found on her flawless face. I sat on the edge of the chair where my mother was sitting. I wanted to ask her some questions, but I didn't want to alert her to the fact that I had been talking with my other siblings about some of her symptoms. I know looks can be deceiving, but I didn't care. To me, my mother was everything. If she said she was fine, then I had to take her word for it.

Almost two years before, my aunt was diagnosed with breast cancer and it had devastated my mother. My mother had six siblings and one of her younger sisters had already died of breast cancer. It was a horrible disease that devastated our family at the time, as we are a very close-knit bunch. I was mad too, my aunt kept this from everyone until she just couldn't hide it anymore. One day it seemed she was a vibrant member of our church choir, and the next she was an invalid with round the clock hospice care. I loved my aunt, but my mother was devastated. Her little sister was dying, and there was not a thing she could do at this point to help but be by her side. When my aunt passed away, I wanted to take all the pain that my mother was feeling on myself. This was her little sister and she wasn't supposed to die first.

When I came home from California, I wanted my mother to have a complete physical, get a mammogram and anything else a woman her age should be expected to have annually. My father was retired but our country's health care system is exceptionally flawed. You can retire at 62 and collect Social Security, but you are not eligible for Medicare until 65 years of age. This means for three years, you either have nothing or you pay thousands of dollars in premiums and starve. This system has failed hardworking, American people who have slaved over jobs – and now cannot even afford to pay to go to the doctors when they are most vulnerable. A solution was needed to help my mom with her health care needs, but what could I do? I thought about going to court just to see if I could be my mother's guardian so that she could be put on my health insurance but that didn't work. The job I worked for didn't honor your parents as a dependent. My mother did what she could to take care of her basic medical needs. My older sister and my mother took a summer job cleaning cottages. This money at least allowed my mother to go to the doctors for her basic needs and pay for prescriptions. I was hearing stories from my sister that our mother would sleep all the way to work and could not really do the work. My sister knew our mother did not even realize how much she was covering for her – but she never said a word, or our mother never would have taken half the money.

I guess warning bells started to go off in my mind because I decided it was time for another conversation with my siblings, this time with our mother included. We started asking her questions about why she was not as active as she use to be, why she was so tired, and why she was sleeping so much. Before we could finish talking to our mother, she started crying. With all of us on the phone, she said these words: "The doctor will probably tell me I have cancer." That hit me like a ton of bricks. I told my mother that we needed to get her to a doctor and find out what was going on. She became very angry; that is the first time I ever heard her raise her voice. She was mad at all of us – she did not appreciate us getting together and talking about her over the phone. I was so hurt I wanted to cry, but I had to remain strong for what I believed would come next. My mother was very upset with all of us, and didn't want to talk at all. I am guessing that she was just very scared of the outcome of her diagnoses. I love my mother with everything in me, so I went and checked on her the next day, regardless of if she wanted me to or not. As she laid there sleeping on the couch, I knew God was looking over us. I knew then, I would do everything I could to help this woman who meant everything to me. Two weeks had gone by since we had the five-way conversation, and it seemed as if my mother's condition did not change at all – she was still sleeping and not feeling well. But this time, my younger sister noticed an odd smell when near our mother – like a bad infection might smell. It was not right, and we had to help her. My mother wouldn't let anyone get near her; she would say, "I am fine. Leave me alone." Unbeknownst to my mother, my younger sister made an appointment with the doctor for her to have a complete checkup. Once we got our mother there, our suspicions were correct; she was very sick. A blood count check was done, and it was discovered by the doctor that my mother hemoglobin levels were at a negative five, and an emergency blood transfusion was critically needed to keep her alive. It was immediate panic for everyone, as she was taken to the hospital directly across from the doctor's office, and directly admitted into the hospital for a blood transfusion. After my mother got undressed, we discovered that the smell that was coming from her was from her breast. The breast tissue had rotted throughout from a cyst that had developed on the inside that grew to the outside; that was why my sister could smell a foul odor around her. The doctor told my sister that they would have to remove our mothers left breast, and she should be fine after the surgery. The pain I felt I had suppressed while I was in California came rushing out at me like a bolt of lightning. I was scared to death, and I could not seem to get air into my lungs. I could not breathe at all, but I had to be strong for my mother. Her operation was a complete success. She appeared to be in minimum pain, and you could see that she was relieved for now. The worst was yet to come. My mother was released from the hospital but I needed to be closer to my mother. I went to work and talked with Human Resource management. I needed to take a leave of absence from work to take care of my mother, and they authorized that.

In mid-August 2002, when my mom was having her follow up after surgery, they discovered she had breast cancer, stage 4. As she prepared herself for what was about to happen inside of her body, I had to also prepare myself for the mental anguish I was about to endure. I was not ready at all for this, so I prayed, and I prayed for the strength to take care of my mother – mentally and physically. I was a total mess inside, but my job was to hold things together for my mother. I was physically weak every time I thought about what she was going through for such a long time before we even knew that she was sick; it would take me to my knees. "Dear God, how can I be losing my mother too," I thought. I prayed, and I prayed that God would save her from that disease called cancer. My mother stayed in the hospital for about a week before she was allowed to come home. The oncologist appointment was set up right away. I was ready to see my mom through this – whether or not my sisters would or could help me – I didn't care. Whether or not my mother could or couldn't afford chemotherapy, I didn't care. I just want my mom to be healed – by any means necessary. I was hurt – so hurt – by what my mother was going through. I thought, "How could I have left her, and gone off on a job assignment to California while she was here going through a private hell of her own?!" Chemo started right away after her surgery. I remember meeting the oncologist – he was a nice-looking, well-spoken man who appeared to be too young. To me, that meant inexperienced, so I really didn't want him to touch my mother. I was taught that with age, comes wisdom. I thought that my mom would need an older doctor with experience instead of a younger doctor with good looks. Nevertheless, I just wanted them to save my mother's life. I was with her at her first chemo treatment, and we got to speak with the doctor about her diagnoses and what effects the chemical would have on her body as she endured the sessions. My question to him was, "Would my mother live through all the poison that would go through her veins?" I also wanted to know if she could be 100% cured of cancer, and he told me that yes, she could be. I was excited, but I was also very angry that my mother's primary care doctor had never caught the elevations or low blood counts, if he was properly giving her an annual exam. My mother was in for the fight of her life.

I SUPPORT HER

The first full day of chemo, my mother sat for almost four hours while they installed a couple of needles in her so that she could receive the chemo treatments. I was so scared; I looked around and observed about five or six ladies taking chemo treatment as well, but I was looking into their faces and all of them where wearing scarves of different colors so I was assuming they have lost their hair. Would that happen to my mother too? I sat through her first session. She seemed to be very happy at that time; she was now more energetic and carefree again. When we left the oncology office, my mother was very hungry. According to all the pamphlets that she had received, she could no longer eat a lot of the food she used to eat while on chemo. I took her to Quality Sea Food and I bought her a fish plate with hush puppies that was one her favorite places to eat when she didn't feel like cooking. I was feeling a little better about what was happening with my mother she could now drive and do whatever she wanted to do, within reason. If she was happy, I was happy. Her first night at home after having the chemo treatment, something was going on with her – but I went home, as I would be just a phone call away and could get back quickly. I needed to check on my children, feed them and find out what my live-in boyfriend was up to, because he was not being very supportive of me. After I went to bed, my phone rang. It was my father telling me that my mother hadn't slept all night, and she was anxious and sitting up on the side of the bed. I got up and took a quick shower, left my kids and boyfriend in the early hours to go check on my mother. I assumed this was a side effect or an allergic reaction to the chemo treatment causing her to have extreme anxiety. I thought it was very strange that my mother was feeling this way, but I waited until eight o'clock in the morning to call the oncology office. I wanted them to prescribe something that could help her sleep and cope with what she was ingesting into her blood stream. I

I SUPPORT HER

was very scared again for my mother; I was making myself sick with worry. I was informed that it was a normal thing that my mother would experience anxiety and sleeplessness. They scheduled her for three treatments of chemo per week for six weeks. The problem that was on the table was: how would she be able to afford to pay for the chemo with no insurance and no money? The answer was simple – she could not afford it. This weighed heavily on my mind for a few days. I didn't care about nothing or no one all; I wanted was my mother to get well, and to be the vibrant, carefree lady she has always been to me, the family and her friends she loved so much. In my thought process, I asked God to guide me and to please give me a way to help save my mother. I did what I thought was right; I took every single dime I had in my 401k and I paid for my mother's chemo treatments. I didn't care if I sold everything; I had I just wanted my mother cancer free and alive. That was all I needed. My mother's chemo treatments were $450.00 a session. I wanted to make sure she got every treatment she needed. I took her to social security administration building to help fill out the paperwork for Medicaid and SSI. I was baffled the first time she was denied for both of them, even though the doctor had filled out and signed all the paperwork, and she was completely qualified to receive it! Where there was a will there was a way. I was even more determined to save my mother's life. I absolutely hated everyone that could not do their job to help me help my mother. I remember crying myself to sleep, but I couldn't let my mother see me like this. I would go away quietly and cry in a corner. I was feeling defeated everywhere I turned; I had no friends to call and check on me, no family that was helping me try to save our mother. My parents had been living with my sister and she was actually putting them out! I could not believe in this family crisis this could be happening, but no retreating was happening with me! I heard

I SUPPORT HER

that there was a program that could help my parents get another house. I took them to the office to help them fill out paperwork for a new modular home that they could live in so that they wouldn't have to worry about being homeless. That worried my mother so bad she would cry every day with me and my older sister. It was time for my mother's next chemo treatment, and after the second round of chemo my mother had a CT scan which had showed that the cancer had not spread anywhere but it was still in her breast area. I was very happy; I thought that this could actually help my mother if the cancer had not spread to any other parts of her body. I was getting very weak and tired, but I couldn't give up on my mother – ever! I hadn't given up – it was just that I needed my siblings to step up to the plate. I needed help, and they just were not picking up the slack at all. I could not even leave to spend any time with my kids because of my sibling's lack of support. I, like my mother, felt like I had been run over by a truck! The second round of chemo caused my mother to have the same reaction as the first round of chemo, so I asked the doctor what to do to lessen the bad side effects of the chemo she was receiving. Unfortunately, he told me that he could not do anything except prescribe a sleep aid, because fighting advanced stage 4 cancer had to be approached aggressively in order for my mother to live. I became more and more scared of what was happening to my mother. My mother had stopped eating, and she was losing weight at a drastic rate. My mother was a 280 pound, five foot – five inches lady, with a smile that could light up any room in the house. The weight loss scared me the most because it was so fast: 280 pounds down to 190 pounds. I was shook to my core. I asked them what I could give her since she was not eating. I was told to give her Ensure, which was filled with all the protein and vitamins she needed. I was happy that she liked the Ensure; it was all that she would drink because sted like metal to her – yet another horrible side effect of cheduled my mother's chemo treatments for Monday, and Friday so someone could be with her at night and I could spend the night with her on the weekends. I needed her, more than ever, to get well. She was my best friend – and more importantly, she was my mother.

I never had a mammogram, but this encouraged me to see my doctor to start the ball rolling. I scheduled a complete physical, which included having a breast exam and a mammogram as well. I went, but I didn't know what was expected when they told me to undress so that they could lift my large breast on a screen, and then flatten it like a pancake in order to take different views, checking for lumps, cysts and calcifications in my breasts. I was scared and very anxious to know the results of the mammogram. I encouraged all my sisters, family members and friends to do as I had done and go have them checked. Thank God, it was negative for breast cancer. Breast cancer is hereditary and since my Aunt and now my mother had it, I was not going to take getting annual mammograms lightly ever again!

In the early hours of the second week of chemo, my mom called and said she wanted to go to the dollar store and Rose's, which were her favorite places to shop for home goods, undergarments and socks. I decided after we came home from chemo that I would drive her wherever she wanted to go. Unfortunately, my mother became very weak, and her legs where not strong enough to hold her up. I went and rented a wheelchair because she could not stand, let alone walk on her own. I was very scared. I thought to myself, "I need answers, and I need them soon. my mother is not going to be in a wheelchair." I waited until I got my mother in the car, then I pretended that I left my wallet in the chair in the doctor's office so I could go back in without alarming her. I wanted answers! I went back into the office and I saw the doctor. I asked him what and why is my mom so weak that she can't even walk on her on two feet. He immediately started explaining to me that some cancer patients' muscles become very weak and they can't walk on their own anymore, but he assured me that when her chemo is completed, and that stuff is out of her system, she would be able to walk again. I had to believe him even though I knew there was no exact science on each cancer patient's prognosis. I still had to have hope!

My mom's beautiful curly hair was beginning to fall out in patches. I wanted her to feel comfortable in public, so I took her to buy a nice wig. When she tried it on, she hated it at first – I guess she was not used to wearing a wig. But she got used to it, and it became normal. My mother was becoming more and more agitated with herself and others. Lashing out at me for no reason at all, but I had to believe it was just a side effect. I took whatever she needed to say to me, maybe she was mad at the world, and even God for making her go through this. I loved my mother and I would not let her push me away, I continued to do anything to keep her happy, I bent over backwards for my mother and do not regret a minute of it. My father was her biggest agitator, my mother felt like he didn't see her as a woman anymore since she had her breast removed. She felt he did not want to be bothered with her, so she took all her frustration out on him, constantly cursing him out. They had been married for over forty years, and nothing could separate them. This was all part of the process I would later learn; you go through stages of grief with cancer, just like you do with a death of a loved one, and my mother was in the anger stage! I remember one cold day in November, my mother was sitting on the couch and she wanted me to fix her some collard greens. I had never cooked collards a day in my life. I didn't know how to wash them or what meat to use to season them, but that day I learned as she told me step by step. I only made one mistake – nevertheless they were good, and seeing my mother enjoy eating them gave me great pleasure. This was the first real food my mother had eaten in a long time, and I was so happy to see her enjoy it! The nights I spent with my mother where long and were getting increasingly harder on me. I was starting to feel worried again my mother being so agitated all the time. In reality, "agitated" is putting it too nice – she was being downright mean to everyone. One of my sisters was helping out a little and living with them. However, she could not handle our mother and moved out. The whole caretaking process now fell squarely on me. For the most part, my sisters visited our mother and my mother was very receptive and willing to see them. My sister Bernice was a different story. Of course she was welcome, but she knew the rest of us were still angry at her lack of compassion to help. Bernice came by one day and our mother wanted to go shopping at Rose's. Out of pure guilt, Bernice agreed to take her. The trip became a horrible ordeal for my mother. My sister would not help her get into her wheelchair – which she was totally dependent on now. Then she left her in an aisle alone in the store. My mother was not only heartbroken and mad but defeated by this. When I heard my mother tell me what happened, I become outraged by my sister's actions. My sister's version was completely different. When I asked her why she would leave her alone in an aisle, she denied it ever happened. But I knew my mother would not lie to me. In my opinion the lack of empathy my sister was showing was uncalled for. My mother was actually scared to be alone with her now! While my mother continued to decline while on chemo, my sister went on a vacation. I just could not believe that anything was more important than all of us supporting each other and our mother. My mother was now very resentful towards my sister and would not allow her to be near her. I understood, even though it made my caretaking job even more difficult. I loved my mother from a place that is so deep, that I would have walked through a burning building to save her. I was fighting too; I did not want to lose my best friend.

Everything seems to happen at the worst time. I thought my eleven-year relationship was a forever one, as we were basically common law married. However, in the middle of this, he takes a job in Florida for the next year! You would think we would have discussed this first, not asked my permission but at least include me in his decision – but it was not the case. He appeared oblivious to my sadness and pain. As I said earlier, he was not supportive. He was not a giver, but rather a taker – and I felt like he had taken a part of my heart and trampled on it. My children were running amok because I was busy taking care of my mother all the time, and now I had to figure this dilemma out. I had to do something different. I decided to just go home and stay home at night, and I let my father take care of my mother at night. But trust me when I say, I was right back there in the morning after the kids went to school. It seemed to work out a little better for me, but I still wasn't sleeping because I was so worried about my mother. I can remember only one of my cousins visiting me during that time. My cousin, Bell, came and sat with me several times so that I could have someone to talk to. I was very appreciative of her for this because she took time out of her schedule to reassure me that everything was going to be well with my mother. I was so hopeful that what Bell said was true. Only God knew truly how scared I was, and how I was feeling about everything that was happening to my mother and I. Day and night I prayed for God to watch over my mother, and help her make it through this terrible suffering and come through it cancer free. I still had hope – and sometimes, hope and a prayer are all you have to go on. My boyfriend was leaving for his new job, and I honestly was at the point where it could not have been soon enough. He was more of a burden than a partner, and I thought this was very odd since he and my mother had a very loving relationship before she became ill. He was not there for me or my mother when I needed him the most, so honestly, I was hoping he would not return. Maybe it takes something devastating for you to become aware of traits in people that are not admirable. I felt the same way about the rest of my family also. I was the one showing up every day, and nobody else seemed to think to ask, "Do you need some help or a weekend off?" I would never let my mother know these feelings, but I had some bitterness festering inside me for my family's lack of support.

My mother was three weeks into her chemo, and things seem to be okay, her body was getting accustomed to the treatments. I continued to be the dutiful daughter that did whatever she needed me to do; nothing could have changed that! I had completely shut down from my life to continue to fight for my mother's health and welfare. My job was supportive of me, they gave me the leave I needed to take of my mother, but I wasn't getting paid. In the third week of my mother's chemo, I asked the doctor if he could write a note for my job for a stress related illness. The oncologist knew being my mother's full-time nurse was making me physically and emotionally sick. It was something he was more than willing to do, and they immediately drafted a letter for me to take to my job so I could get short term disability. This was not just a job; this was my career. I am – and always have been – very dedicated to my job. Being that I was a valued asset to the company, they were more than willing to help me, as long as they knew I would eventually return. This eased my mind and helped even more with the chemo treatments my mom was having. God was good to me, and I was very thankful for his grace and mercy in this desperate time.

The chemo appeared to be gradually helping my mother, or at least I thought so! In the fourth week of chemo, my mother's weight had dropped even more, and she was looking worse now – paler. She became even more weak. I could not stand to see my mother like this, but I still believed it was getting worse, so she could be cured! My mother was still able to take her own shower and dress herself – probably because she was stubborn about that and did not want any help with her bathing and dressing. Maybe, more now than ever, as she felt disfigured. I still waited outside the door to help her as soon as she was done, or in case of an emergency. One particular day, I was in her bedroom and she had come out of the shower with her robe on. I asked my mom if I could see her wound, just to see if it was healing properly. I was shocked at what I saw. The scar was still not healed, and I could see these little sores and bumps that were obviously infected. I tried not to alarm my mother, but we needed to see the doctor now; I helped my mother get dressed quickly and we drove to the surgeon's office. I needed to know why these sores where on her skin where her breast was removed, why had they not healed, and why had nobody noticed they were obviously infected, and I needed an answer now! When we arrived, I was so nervous and out of breath I could barely talk, but I was not leaving without answers. I just keep thinking, "Dear God, what is going on now?" I was consumed with fear. That fear rapidly turned to reality when the doctor confirmed the cancer was indeed spreading, and the chemo was not working. I was worried, so I had taken my mother to the waiting room so I could hear what the doctor had to say first. After I got this devastating news, I went into the bathroom. Before I could see my mother, I had to get it out of my system. I cried my eyes out until I could pull myself together. Could I be losing my best friend to this disease that took my aunt two years before? How could this be happening?! I pulled myself together and said, "This is not happening today. We are going to continue to fight until we cannot fight any longer!" That same day, I took my mother back to the social security administration building and I helped her get into her wheelchair. I wheeled her in and we took a number. We waited and waited to get called, but I was not leaving without being seen. When we eventually got called to the front, there was a different lady than the one that had helped us on our previous visit. This woman immediately recognized my pain, my eyes were tearful and bloodshot from crying. Could it possibly be, that somehow, someone in this ordeal was going to understand my pain and passion in getting my mother the help she so desperately needed? "This woman was sent by God," is all I could think. She had recently lost her mother to cancer, and was not letting me leave without taking care of all of the paperwork required to get my mother the benefits she had earned! Filling out paperwork was easy because she promised me that she would do everything she could to help my mother receive her rightful benefits. God had placed an angel in that office that day! Shortly after I had filled out the paperwork, a letter came in the mail stating that my mother was now covered under Medicaid, and she would receive her first SSI payment it the beginning of each month. She would also receive the back payments from when she first applied for benefits because she had been refused wrongfully. I informed my mother, and she thought it was too good to be true, but I read the letter and explained it to her. Her smile could have lit up the whole house. I was so happy even though only I knew what the news from the doctor had been that day, my mother was feeling a big victory – and rightfully so. I called and I thanked the young lady for blessing my mother with such good news. I was so happy I didn't have to worry about halting my mother's chemo because of not being able to pay. Not that I wouldn't have found another way; it is amazing where your mind goes when you are fighting to save a loved one's life – bank robbery had momentarily gone through my mind! My mother received almost $1600.00 a month in disability and Medicaid from the state of North Carolina. When her first check came in with her back pay included, she wanted to give me some money to help me with my bills, but I refused to take any money from her. That money was for her and her only. I took her shopping at one of her favorite places, Rose's. With insurance, my mother now was the proud owner of a motorized wheelchair that had a basket in the front. This was new to my mother, so I asked her if she wanted to try to drive alone, and I would walk beside her with my cart. I wanted to try and give her some of her mobility back so she wouldn't feel helpless. I placed her legs inside of the motorized chair, and she took off all by herself. She enjoyed that so much, we stayed inside Rose's for about two hours. I tried my luck by asking my mother if she wanted to get something to eat, and surprisingly, she was up for it. I went to the drive thru at McDonalds and got my mother her large order of fries. I was so excited she ate every last one of them – like a kid in a candy store. I was so impressed; I got a glimmer of hope that my mother might actually be feeling better. We bought more Ensure to drink for added protein and vitamins and she was beginning to feel better and eating a little more every day. I was also starting to feel better and eating a lot more. I had a lost my appetite from the stress of the situation. I started thinking really positively as my mother was surprising me every day with some small milestone.

In early November, it was starting to get really cold and my mother appeared to be around 140, or maybe 145 pounds. This was about half of what her weight had been prior to cancer. I decided my mother and I needed to go get her some warm clothes and a nice coat that she could get in and out of herself. We had another wonderful day, and I was feeling happy, even though things were not what they appeared to be. My sisters called our mother from time to time to check on her, but only one of my siblings took time out of her schedule to come and visit at night. This gave me time to relax and go home to check to see how my kids where doing. They understood and all they wanted was for their grandma to get well. My siblings were not supporting me like I would have thought, but maybe they were not strong enough to handle the stress. I did not openly let them know I thought they were not supporting my efforts to heal our mother enough because my mother would have heard about it, and she did not need any added stress. I could be wrong, but I felt like that often enough to reflect back on it and still see it the same way. My oldest brother, Willie, had gotten into trouble in Maryland and went to prison for almost 15 years, so he was not at home. Of course, he couldn't help out but he kept in contact with our mother through letters and calls. I remember that my mother even while fighting for her life would send my brother money for his canteen and his personal needs. I remember the letter she wrote to my brother telling him that she was sick and that this may be the last letter she might write him. I didn't see the contents of the letter but it was very emotional for my brother being incarcerated and not able to see our mother. I know he wanted to hug her and comfort her but sometimes it just is not possible. He may have been a bad boy – nothing violent – but he was a good son and loved our mother dearly too. One weekend, my mother wanted to visit her uncle, but it was about a two-hour drive. Nevertheless, my father and I drove my mother where she wanted to go. My mother never would have gone without me; by this time my father was really getting on her nerves. My mother was extremely exhausted when she got home, I was also extremely tired but I had to get my mother in the house, help her undress, shower and down for bed.

Monday was her next scheduled chemo treatment. I was very worried now, because after so many chemo treatments, it was time to check on the progress. I had not heard when that would be. The doctor had already decided not to do chemo that day, and when we arrived, they sent us to the hospital for a CT scan instead. I was anxious to find out the result, every second felt like eternity while we were waiting for the results. I needed to know so that I could prepare myself for whatever the doctors told me. I waited for the doctor the next day to call and after what felt like an eternity he did. He wanted my mother to come into the office to discuss her test results, so she got dressed and I drove her to see him. It was her time to go into the doctor's office to hear the results of her CT scan, and what her oncologist was explaining was about my mother's quality of life – not her progress. I didn't understand. What was he was trying to say? I finally asked him to be more specific. I wanted to know if all that poison that was entering into my mother's system was helping her or was it a waste of her time? I needed to know; my nerves was already shot, and it was like he was beating around the brush. I lost my temper with my mother's oncologist, I asked him to be straight forward and he was still beating around the bush and I felt like I just had to say, "Enough bullshit! What exactly are you trying to say in plain English?" He then began to explain to me that the cancer had not spread and it was a good possibility that she could make it, but her quality of life would be compromised. I began understanding that the chemo that my mother was enduring was not really curing her, but it was helping her to stay alive. What I was also understanding was that my mother would not be able to do the things she used to do, such as walk and drive. I was shocked, as this was not what the oncologist said would happen after chemo. I was sad. I felt that I was letting my mother down. At least there was a beacon of hope: the cancer had not spread into any other parts of her body. I had to take this news as a blessing and not a curse, my mother was going to live but would be an invalid. At this point, this was much better than my mother dying.

It was now the beginning of the holiday season, and I wanted to plan something – a nice Thanksgiving dinner. All my mother's kids and grandchildren could come visit, sit and just have a good time. I wanted to at least try to bring the family back together. I had made my mother my priority and no one else had, but I was not going to let my mother know this. Thanksgiving dinner was filled with mixed emotions, my mother was happy, even though I could tell she felt very sick. I was so happy she did eat some food. Some of my siblings and other family came, but not everyone. I was happy my mother didn't notice who was missing. After our Thanksgiving celebration, I was really upset that my mother's siblings did not come by. All my life I remembered my mother taking the time to go visit all her family whenever they were under the weather, and this how they treat her! This infuriated me, but I had to focus on the bigger picture and not let them take my energy from me.

It was early December now; my mom wanted a Christmas tree in the corner by the fireplace I can't remember who put it up – me or the grandkids – but we had a beautiful tree decorated with lights and Christmas balls. My mom was still having chemo treatments, but they were not as frequent as they were before so I was able to relax a little. I could take enough time to go home for a few hours to clean my house and just sleep. I still needed to be with my mother as much as I possibly could. My great nephew, Talib, was born in year 2001, before my mother was diagnosed with breast cancer so she got to take care of him. She loved her grandsons especially my other nephew, Raphael; she had raised him from age two until he was a grown man. Now Talib was her baby. He was almost one, but she still tried to hold him and keep him until my niece moved out with him. I think that hurt my mother, not to have her grandson to love, hold, and tend to – as if her illness was contagious!

When I think back, I realize why my mother kept her illness a secret. She didn't want anyone to worry. She wanted to spend as much time with us as she possibly could, in whatever was left of her best life. Chemo had taken a toll on my mother's health, but she was determined and she was a fighter. I, on the other hand, was seeing everything from a different perspective. I was watching my mother fade away to nothing more than skin and bones. There had been a lot of mornings I would fall down on my knees and pray, through my tears, for God to give her strength and remove my weakness. I had suddenly become very depressed. I felt like I was losing my mind, but I could not let my mom see me in this state. I pulled myself up every day to try my best to keep my mother alive.

Christmas was approaching rapidly, and I wanted my mother to have the best Christmas ever. I would run out when my mother had company to do some Christmas shopping, I thought a little retail therapy to give my mother a surprise could not hurt. Elizabeth City had just got a new jewelry store and I wanted to buy my mother a beautiful watch and some diamond earrings. I went into the store and I found a very nice watch, it wasn't too expensive and I got some diamond studs on sale. I was very

I SUPPORT HER

excited and I wanted my mom to wear them, but I had to wait to see them on her until Christmas. I came back to my mother's that afternoon and her sisters were there, which was fairly unusual. I went in, and I wanted to check to see if anyone had fixed or brought my mother something to eat. My mother said "I am not hungry, feed yourself." That made me worry even more at least if she was eating, I would feel happy. I had lost weight myself, from being so stressed. I didn't care, all I wanted was my mother to be okay. My appearance was the last thing I cared about at that time. I didn't have any support system just me and my mother. Occasionally someone would come over and sit with her but they sure didn't do anything but sit there. Christmas time was a week away and I was still shopping for my mom and my two kids. I bought them everything they wanted, and then some. I was still praying that my mom would get better, and it seemed as if she was – or so I thought. My mother was still going to chemo treatments, but the amount of chemo she was taking in had been reduced; therefore, it was time for them to give her another CT scan. The showed that my mother's cancer was still not spreading, but it was still stage four cancer and she had to endure more chemo. I knew that my mom was a fighter, and she would endure it as long as she needed too.

Christmas had arrived, and it was so cold that day I didn't want to get out of bed. I had turned the heat up, but my two kids would not let me sleep because they wanted to open their Christmas presents. All I could hear was the tearing of wrapping paper and them saying, "Thanks, Mom! How did you know I wanted this?" I got up and I took a shower so that I could go and help my mother with whatever she needed me to do, but before I could get down to my mother's house my dad called to find out what time I was coming to help. After my mother ate some breakfast, I gave her the Christmas presents from me. She loved the watch more than anything else, so I put it on her and the smile on her face was priceless. Everyone came to see her and brought presents that day. She was all smiles. I could tell my mother was getting sleepy – she kept nodding off. My mom could sleep anywhere and through any noise. I was just happy that she was happy.

Two weeks into the new year, my mother was not feeling well at all; she was very irritated and extremely weak. I had spent the whole night with her because she couldn't sleep. I was exhausted. Something was terribly wrong, and I was sick with worry – but I sat through it all until she finally went to sleep. I, too, fell asleep; and when I woke my mom was still asleep. I didn't want to wake her, so I quietly left and went home to check on my kids. I just wanted to make sure they had gotten up and were dressed to go to school. I knew that once they left, I was going to lay down and get a quick nap before I took a shower and returned to my mother's house. I took a brief nap and was awakened by a phone call from my father. He needed me to come quickly because my mother had an accident because she couldn't make it to the bathroom. I told my father to give me a few minutes to get up and dressed. I only lived six minutes away from my parents, so I could be there quickly. When I got into the house, my mother apologized and I felt there was no need for her to apologize to me – I was a baby once and she had to change me. I only did what I had to do, and that was to clean her up and put some fresh underclothes on with her pajama outfit so that she could lounge around for the day. I cancelled the chemo session that was scheduled that day. My mom was tired and very weak, and I didn't want her to go. It was also extremely cold and I didn't want her exposed with her weakened immune system. We sat and watched a gospel show on television; it was a good sermon that made me have hopes for my mother. My mother was sitting and nodding her head as she listened to the preacher and then I heard her say "Amen" and "Thank you, Jesus" in such a calm manner as if she also had hopes. I was feeling very happy – but as always, a nagging sadness too. Late into the evening, my mother's siblings stopped by and had my mother laughing about what they used to do when they were kids. While listening to their stories, I realized by my mother being the oldest, she had literally raised her siblings. My grandmother had passed away, and my mother helped her father by doing all the cooking and cleaning. I knew my mother was a caring and nurturing person because she took care of everyone. Now I realized why she made it look so easy. She loved it, and everyone loved her for it. It was getting really late, and I needed to slip away and cook my young adults something to eat. I left for a short time to cook them dinner and to make sure they were ok. I was glad now, that my boyfriend was gone. I felt like he added more stress when my mother was sick, and I did not need that. I was doing a fine job of falling deeper and deeper into depression, and I needed to figure out how to remain strong for my mother.

It was Monday January 23, 2003, I will never forget that day. I was more exhausted than ever. I had stayed up with my mother while she had her worst night since she had started chemo. Her anxiety was so bad; I was scared, helpless and did not know how to help. My mother could not be still, she was up and down and extremely agitated. I was so worried about her, so I stayed there until we all went to sleep. The next morning, I left to go back home while she was sleeping. I only left to get a shower and make sure the kids where okay. I had not been home but one hour when my baby sister called and said that my mom had messed in her pants, and she wanted me to come and clean her up, so I did just that. I came back, within an hour, cleaned her up and got her into the living room. But something just didn't seem right to me. When I sat her in the chair, she slumped over I thought she was just too weak to sit up, but it was more – and I was scared. I picked up the phone and called an ambulance to get her to the hospital. My mother had lost so much weight and was so weak, they immediately called her doctor. The doctor told the emergency room to do a chest CT scan STAT! The CT scan showed that my mother's cancer had spread throughout her lungs. This was all surreal to me. How could they have not seen this last month? Mom's cancer had spread to her lungs. I couldn't take it. I had to leave the room as the doctor was informing me and my sisters that my mother had only a short time to live. I was devastated at what was being told to me! My mother's oncologist told me last month that my mother was getting better when, in fact, she was getting worse. What was even worse is, my mother's primary care doctor was asking the family should we resuscitate, and I yelled out, "Yes!" He then proceeded to ask me why I wanted my mother to be resuscitated, when there was no hope of survival for her. I was so angry I wanted to kill this man. The fact that she was at the end stage of life had not even sunk in, and this doctor is asking us for a split-second decision. I screamed at him, "This is my mother, not yours." My mother stayed in the hospital from then, until her last breath. The first few hours, I was so devastated I could not go see her. I was enraged at her doctors; I was angry and disappointed. I felt like they had been lying to me. That was not the case, and I should have researched a little myself or even called a support group, but I did not think of these things when I was consumed with healing my mother. The primary care doctor was terrible, but I do know now, that when breast cancer spreads to other parts of your body, it can literally happen in weeks. Metastatic breast cancer is horrible, and my mother's oncologist was doing everything possible in 2002 to cure her. We all took turns staying with her. She was on a heavy dose of morphine, so she didn't know that we were there, but God had the last say so. January 27, 2003, my mother was called home to be with the Lord around one o'clock in the morning. I received the phone call from my sister Bernice. We had to almost curse her out to get her to stay with our mother, but she did. I arrived at the hospital around 1:30 that morning to say goodbye. It was the most painful thing I have ever been thru in my life. Thinking back, I was happy to have spent six months with her laughing, crying and shopping together. The experience of losing a mother to breast cancer made me realize how important breast cancer screening is for me, my siblings, my friends, and all women. We buried my mother on February 1, 2003. She was so beautiful, and her skin was flawless laying as though she was asleep.

These memories will always be forever stamped in my heart.

CHAPTER 3

From The Pit to Promise

"My Journey from Homelessness to Home"

by: Kenesa Bowe

In November of 2018, I was living in a small town of North Carolina called Elizabeth City. Elizabeth City is a limited place where the only major attractions in town are the Coast Guard Base, My Alum and the illustrious Elizabeth City State University, and Walmart. I lived in Elizabeth City for 17 years and lived in North Carolina my entire life – and I felt stuck. The town didn't have many resources and it was very constrained.

I was living in a low-income community and most people that lived there were not motivated to work or living productive lives. When I would step outside of my door, I would see people sitting outside from the time that I would leave to go to work. Those same individuals would still be outside when I would come back home from work. I thought to myself, "I have four people who are looking up to me. As a mother of four, I know

I need to do something different from what I'm doing, but I just don't know where to begin."

My faith in God was strong and I always knew that God had a greater purpose for my life. But there were times where I wondered when my life would change for the better. I knew that all my experiences were testing of my faith and building my character as a person. I used to always ask God, "How strong do you need me to be for my purpose?" I couldn't understand why my children and I had to go through so much, and it still wasn't letting up. I would always tell my children, "God is going to get us out of this! He has something greater for us!" After a while, they started to doubt that was even true because our lives were at a standstill. But I continued to pray, seek God and listen to his instructions.

I was a struggling, single mother with a master's degree. I couldn't fathom why I wasn't successful and couldn't get out of my situation. "What ever happened to the American Dream that I was told about before enrolling into college?", I thought. I searched the internet for years, looking for better opportunities for me to provide for my family. But unfortunately, in my town and surrounding areas, it's not about what you know, but who you know.

At that time, I was contracted through an Insurance company selling supplemental insurance. I had been with the Insurance company for about 6 months already and was not making enough money to sustain my household. The insurance company was a fully based commission corporation. So, if you didn't sell anything, you didn't make any money. I began to get behind significantly on my bills, including my rent.

I SUPPORT HER

My oldest son, Kemarri was struggling in school and had fallen behind. He had lost his motivation and only attended school just to have something to do and somewhere to go during the week. He was working at a nearby barbershop on the weekends but had recently got fired from that job for being disrespectful. He felt as if his life was falling apart.

Kemarri texted me one day and said that he needed to talk to me about something. I immediately got worried because I thought that he was in trouble at school. Kemarri came home from school and handed me 2 documents and stated that he wanted to attend one of the programs. One of the programs was a military school in Salemburg, NC. That one piqued my interest for Kemarri because I thought that he needed a change of scenery. We contacted the school and completed the application. I informed some of Kemarri's family that he would be leaving to go to military school in January.

In December of 2018, I went to pay my rent like I usually did around the 3rd of each month, to ensure that it was on time. My mother was in the car with me and I remember telling her, "let me go drop this money order in the box right now before I forget." I had been living in the apartment for 5 years and never had any issues with my payment not being received. Therefore, I dropped my money order in the drop box of the leasing office. About a week and a half later, I received a letter on my door stating that my rent was past due and that I needed to pay it by a certain date.

I contacted my landlord and explained to her that I dropped my money order off as I had done years before with no issues. My landlord claimed that she didn't see my money order and demanded me the pay the rent and the late fees. Me being on a limited income, I didn't know where

I was going to get the money from because I wasn't making any working for the insurance company. I called my cousin and explained to her my situation and she loaned me the money. I got a money order and took it to my landlord. While in the office, my landlord took my money order and said, "Hold on a minute let me check something." My landlord gave me my money order back and informed me that I needed to come up with at least $130 more dollars of fees. Although $130 may not be a lot of money to some people, it was way more than I had to give. I couldn't ask my cousin for more money because I had just asked her, and I knew that she was going through her own struggles at the time.

Eventually, I got further behind on the bills. Everything that I tried to do to get out of my situation, was not working. I received a letter from my landlord stating that if they didn't receive the additional fees, they would file for an eviction. I immediately became concerned and anxiety filled my body, as I began to worry and doubt myself. Suddenly, God reminded me of the vision that he showed me years ago. In that vision was limitless opportunities, abundance of favor, love and grace, and "Purpose" fulfillment. My heart rate began to slow down, my breaths became longer, and my faith strengthened. In that moment, I declared to the Lord that I would "trust Him" and be obedient to his will. I said to God, "If it's in your will, then allow me to stay." God responded, "You are released, Go!" I had waited several years to hear that. I attempted to leave Elizabeth City 2 times before, but I was not able to leave.

I gathered my children together to discuss what God said. I told them that it was our season to move and I wasn't sure which direction to go. I was going to be obedient and take steps by getting boxes and packing our belongings. I reminded my children that God has been preparing us for this moment and all the dreams of moving were about to happen. My children had many questions and concerns and although they were excited, they were fearful as well. I stated to my children, "This journey we are about to take won't be easy, but it will be worth it. Just follow me as I follow God's instructions." I began to depend on God with my all.

A few days later, I received knock at my door. I opened the door and it was the County Sherriff with an eviction notice. I read the letter and it stated that we had to leave the premises by January 11th, 2019. My son walked up behind me and asked, "Ma, who was that?" I turned to look at him and responded, "It was the Sherriff with eviction papers." Kemarri looked at me as if he was confused, and I explained to him what eviction meant. Kemarri became fearful and asked, "Ma, what are we going to do? Where are we going to go?" I looked at him and calmly responded, "I don't know, but I'm not worried because I know that God's got us!"

In the meantime, we were preparing to send my oldest son Kemarri to military school. His family and some of my family assisted in getting him the things that he needed for military school. Kemarri was so excited to go but nervous at the same time. He would be leaving his family behind, and there was much uncertainty of what would happen to us. Kemarri knew that he needed a change. I promised him that his brother, sisters and I would be okay, and that God had us covered. We took Kemarri to Salemburg, NC for military school on January 5th, 2019 and it was a very emotional day.

I knew that we had to leave but I was unsure of which direction to go to. I reached out to a few family and friends that lived in the Raleigh area, to ask if they knew of any apartments for rent or jobs where I could apply. Unfortunately, none of them were able to help me. I even contacted

I SUPPORT HER

several schools in Raleigh to ask about the enrollment process for son Khyleed, and my daughters KaRyzma and Kelaiah.

Later that evening, I was on one of my social media sites and noticed a funny post from one of my associates, (who I will refer to as Ms. C) from a church that I use to attend. I decided to comment on her post with a joke. Then she sent a message to me through my inbox asking how me and my children were doing. I began sharing with her what we were currently going through and informed her that we had to leave. I also told her that I really didn't know where to go so I had been trying to relocate to Raleigh.

I really didn't want to go to Raleigh because that was the go-to place where everyone from Elizabeth City or my hometown would move to. I only attempted to relocate there because I had family and friends there and I thought that it would be easier to move there. I was still trying to play it safe and fear had crept in. I was afraid to take that leap of faith to move to another state. But God had other plans. He wanted to take me outside of my comfort zone.

Ms. C stated that I should come to Northern Virginia with her and her daughter. She stated that she would talk to her daughter about it and let me know. I asked Ms. C, "Are you sure that you have enough room for me and my family?" Ms. C replied, "Yes, it should be fine. We will work it out." Ms. C contacted me and stated that she talked to her daughter and that she was okay with us coming to stay with them until we got on our feet. Ms. C started contacting me every day sending me all kinds of resources such as numbers to the local schools, Department of Social Services, and storage units. This was going to be my first big move and I didn't know where to start, so Ms. C's help was appreciated.

I SUPPORT HER

It was January of 2019 and as soon as I was able to file my taxes, I did. My accountant asked me if I wanted to get a loan on my taxes and I told him, "Yes!" I was able to get a $2500 loan on my taxes which came back the day after I filed. So, I paid my tithes which was $250 and left the rest for our new journey.

Ms. C would call and ask what I did that day in preparation for the move. I was still hesitant because I knew that that Ms. C's daughter could be very bratty and jealous when it comes to her mother. Years ago, my sister moved in with Ms. C and her daughter after moving from our hometown to start a new life. My sister informed me of her experiences with Ms. C and her daughter. But I thought, "That was years ago and maybe she has matured by now." I had to constantly encourage myself that everything would be okay. Ms. C was encouraging me the to take different steps daily to make the transition smooth. I said to myself, "God is leading us to a new place for a new life and as long as he is with us, we will be okay. "

I contacted a storage company closest to Ms. C's daughter's town house. The storage company was running a promotion sale for the new year, so I was able to get my first month's rent free. I was excited about that. I contacted a nearby storage place that rented U-Haul's and he gave me an estimate. I set me alarm for 2:00am so that my oldest daughter and I could go to Wal-Mart in the middle of the night to get boxes for the move. When my alarm went off at 2:00am, my daughter and I went to Wal-Mart to get boxes for the move. We got some big and some medium size boxes. I contacted a co-worker, Char, and asked her if she could drive my car and my girls to Virginia for me while I drove the U-Haul. Char agreed to do it.

I SUPPORT HER

I went in the middle of the night because that was the only time where you can grab boxes after they stock the shelves. I also didn't want anyone to see us or know that we were moving. I was not ashamed of what we were going through. I just didn't want anyone to try to talk me out of moving, like they had done on the past. I've learned that you don't share your dreams and goals with anyone because they will try to discourage you from what God told you to do.

KaRyzma and I came home and took the boxes inside. I woke up at 8:30am and begin to pack up the kitchen. We had already thrown a lot of stuff away that we weren't planning to take with us. I wanted to pack lightly because we were going into a new season and I knew that we would get new furniture. I paid a friend of mine to take my old television, entertainment center, sofa and loveseat to the landfill. My children and I worked hard to get all rooms packed up and things thrown out so that we could have a smooth transition. I asked my neighbor if he could help us get the big items to the U-Haul on tomorrow since that was the day we were planning to move. My neighbor agreed to help us. We spent the rest of the day packing and labeling boxes and moving stuff to the front room by the door.

That evening, I talked with my children about the plan for the next day. Khyleed started asking a lot of questions about the move and where we were going to be staying. I could tell that he was very nervous and unsure about things. I went to his room to have a talk with him and asked him what was he afraid of? Khyleed responded that he didn't want us to fail. I reminded Khyleed of the times that we use to talk about leaving this town to go somewhere with better opportunities. I encouraged Khyleed that to be strong and courageous in this next season of our lives. I knew that he was struggling with all of this especially since his brother was gone to military school and he felt like he was alone. Although Kemarri and Khyleed are brothers, there are also best friends.

The next morning, I woke up and said a prayer for my family. I asked God to make the transition smooth as possible. I contacted Char to ask her if she was ready to meet me to pick the U-Haul? She stated that she was on her way. When we got there, the man asked me more detailed questions about where we were going. The total was a lot cheaper than the price they gave me the day before. I started thanking God for the favor that He was showing me and my family. We got the U-Haul and headed to my apartment.

The children, Char, my neighbor and myself began to move items to my car and U-Haul. I knew that we couldn't take everything with us, so I gave 2 of our televisions away to our neighbors. Once we finished putting our stuff in the truck and car, we locked up and left. I had a certain time to get to the storage unit before they closed for the day. Char drove my car with my girls KaRyzma and Kelaiah, and Khyleed rode with me in the U-Haul. That was my first experience getting and driving a U-Haul and getting a storage unit.

It took us 3 ½ hours to drive to Northern Virginia. I felt so excited and free. We arrived at the storage unit just in time. I signed my storage lease and got my key. It started to rain as we begin to move all the items in that we weren't taking to Ms. C's daughter's home. Once we got all the items in, we locked the storage and headed to Ms. C's. When we arrived Ms. C and her daughter, Ari, were home. They welcomed us in, and we took our boxes to our room. It was a small room for 1 person, but we were going to make it work. I brought my mattress so that the girls could sleep with me and Ms. C said that Khyleed could sleep on the couch downstairs.

After we moved our belongings in the room, I told Ms. C and Ari that I had to take Char and Khyleed back to Elizabeth City. I was taking Khyleed back to stay with his cousin for a week because he wanted to finish his semester. Khyleed had to take his "End of Course" tests before he moved with us for good. I also had to take Char back to her car and blessed her for helping us.

I was so tired on the way back that my face began to tremble. It was about two o'clock in the morning, and my body was shutting down. I began to pray and ask the Lord to get us there safely. We arrived at our destination and parking was a major issue there. I dropped the girls off at the door and I parked my car by the office and walk all the way to Ari's home. My girls and I were exhausted. We took our showers and went to bed.

The next morning, we got ready to get KaRyzma registered in school. KaRyzma was nervous more than anything. I completed her forms and the school stated that it would take a few days before they were going to call us with her start date. So we left her new school and went to the high school, where Khyleed would be attending, to get his paperwork started. The advisor gave me the forms to complete and asked me to bring Khyleed with me when he returned to enroll him.

We went back to Ari's place to complete paperwork. Ari had a little dog, and me, KaRyzma and Khyleed are apprehensive of dogs. Every time we went to the house, KaRyzma would "clam up." The first night, Ms. C and Ari were encouraging to KaRyzma letting her know that the dog wouldn't harm her. But as days went on, Ms. C and Ari became brutally mean with their words to KaRyzma.

Ari didn't have a kitchen table in the home, so we had to eat our meals in the living room using the coffee table. One time we were eating, and the dog literally jumped on KaRyzma while she was sitting on the couch. KaRyzma was afraid was unable to finish her food. Ari and Ms. C began to taunt KaRyzma by saying we are not going to keep him in his cage just because you are scared. They told her that she couldn't eat in the room and if she was hungry, she had to eat downstairs. There were a few nights that KaRyzma would cry and not eat dinner because she was afraid of the dog. It angered me as a mother! To hear them treating her like that, they were literally bullying her. "Two grown women bullying a child?" I thought to myself. But I remained quiet because I needed somewhere to stay, and I knew that I was in Ari's home.

I talked with KaRyzma one night and prayed with her. I told her, "After today, you will no longer fear the dog." The next day we went down for breakfast and KaRyzma asked me to pick the dog up so that she could rub him. I picked him up and KaRyzma began to rub the dog. After a while she became more comfortable with him. We received a call from the school, and they gave a start date for KaRyzma to start. I took KaRyzma to school and she didn't want me to leave her at first, but I told her that she was going to have a great day.

I went back to Ari's and began to update my resume and apply for jobs online. Ms. C would get down and want to talk, so I would. She would talk about the church members and pastor where we used to attend in the past. She would discuss what happened and why she stopped attending. I would encourage her to have a conversation with them to address her issues so that she could move forward. I could tell that Ms. C was dealing with a lot of hurt from the past because she would get so angry each time, she would bring certain things up.

Ms. C would ask me what I wanted to do and what was my goals, and I was afraid to share certain things with her because although she invited me in her home, I didn't trust her completely. Ms. C would share her goals and visions with me, and I would encourage her to follow them and not to wait. I would share only a few goals but not the big ones, because I didn't want it to turn into a competition.

But for several years, I wanted to become a Life Coach. I was already a Published Author, but I wanted to add Life Coaching to my resume as well. I had a vision that God gave me years ago and I was ready to move forward with those goals. One day while on LinkedIn, I saw a request for a man that I didn't know. I clicked on his profile and saw that he was Certified Life Coach. I accepted his friend request and told him that I noticed he was a Life Coach and that I wanted to know how I could become one. He sent me the link to the school that he attended and encouraged me to apply. I made sure that saved the link so that when I was ready, I could attend a class.

A week after the move, it was time to pick Khyleed up from Elizabeth City. He had completed his semester and his End of Course test. I picked Khyleed up and was hoping that he was excited about our new beginning as I was. But Khyleed was very quiet on the ride to Northern Virginia. I asked Khyleed, "Are you okay?" He responded, "I'm just nervous, that's all."

The next day, I took Khyleed to school to enroll him and the Enrollment Advisor gave me a hard time about enrolling Khyleed because we didn't have a lease stating that we lived in Virginia. We had to get a form signed by Ari and notarized in order to keep him enrolled. Khyleed returned home from school and stated that he had a long day. I asked him, "What happened?" Khyleed replied, "They made me wait most of the morning in the office and then they took me around to tour the school."

The first few days were filled with laughter and fun. But after a week, things in the home changed quickly. Ari was in the military and worked in D.C. She would call during the day to talk to her mother and would get upset when her mother would tell her that we were talking or out handling business. If I went out to go somewhere whether it was to the store or looking for homes, or resources, Ms. C wanted to go with me. I understood that she was trying to help me but after a while, it seemed as if she was trying to control me. I would tell Ms. C, "Please let me go out on my own so I can figure the city out for myself. I don't want Ari to think that I'm trying to take her mother time away from her, because I'm not." I would make sure that I thanked Ari and Ms. C every day. I wanted them to know that I appreciated everything that they were doing for my family by letting us stay with them. I even would send them money to their cash apps even when they didn't ask for it.

Ari and Ms. C never asked for any rent money but when I got blessed, I would always bless them with some money. As I continued to apply for jobs, I decided to apply to be a driver for Door Dash. I thought it would at least keep some money in my pockets and we could learn the city while serving our community. When I got my starter package to begin door dash, I was so excited to start my first job in a new area. Although door dash wasn't a full-time job, I was still humbled and appreciative. I went to tell Ms. C the good news, and she didn't seem to be happy about it at all. It was almost as if she was trying to steal my joy. We had so many talks about working towards our goals and having to crawl before you walked. Anything that I would do that moved me closer to my goals, Ms. C would try to discount it or talk me out of it.

The first time my children and I went out to do Door Dash, Ms. C and Ari decided to go out to do Uber Eats. While we were out dashing, Ms. C called us several times to see where we were at and asking how much money we made. It was like they were trying to compete with me and my children. We continue to dash throughout the week, trying to make sure that I wasn't burning through all my savings. But my money was getting rather low and I needed a job soon.

Every morning I would take my son to the bus stop to make sure that we had our one-on-one time, that was my time to check in with him to make sure that he was doing okay with the new school and environment. He stated that he was having some issues at school and wasn't quite fitting in. I encouraged him to try not to fit it and be a leader instead. I told him that the right people would come along and be a real friend to him. On top of that stress, Khyleed was dealing with Ms. C and Ari making crass remarks to him daily about his weight or his complexion.

Khyleed told me that one night when I was upstairs, Ms. C and Ari were calling him ugly and black. I got so angry with them both because I found it ironic that they could insult him about his complexion, and he had the same complexion as them. I felt like it was an attack on me because they knew that my children were my heart and I would do anything for them. They really wanted to say things to me to hurt my feelings, but they weren't bold enough, so they began attacking my children behind my back.

I SUPPORT HER

I started receiving my mail at Ari's and my bills were piling up and my credit was dropping drastically. I received a letter from my old apartment with a bill inside. I wanted to decrease my bills and increase credit, so I decided to pay one bill at a time. I began to make payments on it until I paid them in full. I asked them to send me a letter stating that completed my payment and owed a $0 balance.

Ari's community had a gate and if you were not inside of the gate by 7pm, you needed to get a visiting pass to get in or you could not get in the gate. Every night, Ms. C would make it a big deal about me getting a visitor's pass for my car. Ms. C stated, "They are not going to keep giving you a pass every night. After a while they will began to question if you stay here. So, I would make sure that if the children and I needed to go to the store or went out for food, that we were in the gate by 7:00pm. At one time Ari would save her spot for my car so that I didn't need to geta pass. I would thank her for that because I knew that she didn't have to do that.

There were times where Ms. C would park Ari's car in her spot so that I would have to get a pass for the night. Ms. C had a car, but it was not working properly. Sometimes Ms. C would park her car in the parking garage at the train station, which was about 5 miles away. There were a few times where Ms. C would tell me that her car needed to get fixed and how much it was going to cost her. I would just listen and stay silent because I knew that it was her way to manipulate me to get her car fixed. I know that I wasn't paying rent, but I was sending them both money through their cash app's, cooking for them at times and buying supplies for the house.

Ms. C knew that I didn't have a full-time job and that what I was making delivering food was not enough to take care of my children and I and her car too. Several times I gave Ms. C's car a jump just so that she could move it around from one space to another. There were times when Ms. C would tell me that I should park my car in the parking garage at the train station and she would take me to my car in the morning. I asked, "How would I take my children to the bus stop and school each morning?" Ms. C replied, "I can take you to your car every morning or I can help take them to the bus stop and school." I knew that it was a trap and I wouldn't agree to parking my car in the parking garage. Ms. C was trying to control us, and our movements and I wasn't falling for the manipulation.

Most days I would just stay to myself in the room especially when the children were in school. I was unable to get Kelaiah in school because there were no schools in the area that took 3 years old's without having to pay tuition. So, after taking Khyleed to the bus stop and KaRyzma to school, Kelaiah and I would eat breakfast and sleep until it was time to for Khyleed to come home.

I received my first letter from Kemarri. I was so happy to hear from him. I had covered him daily in prayer, hoping that all was well with him. In his letter, he wrote how much he missed his family. Kemarri stated that his outlook on life had changed and he wanted to be a better person. I was so happy to hear that. Towards the end of the letter he wrote that he wished that we would move out of Elizabeth City and moved to a more productive area. I smiled with tears in my eyes as I knew that his prayers had already been answered. I responded to Kemarri's letter and informed him that we relocated to Northern Virginia.

It had been a month since Kemarri was taken to military school. The school did not allow phone calls until after the students were there for a month. I had to mail Kemarri a phone card so that he could call home to speak to me every week. Kemarri called us and we were so excited to hear from him. We wanted to know everything that he had done, and experienced and what it was like for him in there? Kemarri stated that he was so excited to read in the letter that we moved. He said that he began to cry when he got the letter and saw the address. Kemarri told us that he had a friend in the school that became like a brother to him. Kemarri also stated that he couldn't wait to see us for family day, and he had a lot to share with us that he couldn't share over the phone.

My children and I left to visit Kemarri for family day. The students gave a presentation for the families and it was amazing to see Kemarri in front of the line. After the presentation the cadets were able to leave for a few hours with their families. Kemarri and his friend decided on the restaurant they wanted to go to. So, we went and while I was there, I met Kemarri's friend's mother. Kemarri and his friend told us about some of the things that they witnessed which was very disturbing. They told us that a few guys tried to commit suicide the first week. I began to pray for his mind and his soul while he was in there. I asked God to protect him and not to allow him to get swayed to do anything negative. I was very concerned for Kemarri because I knew that he would allow peer pressure to get the best of him. I asked him if he wanted to continue the journey and he responded, "Yes!"

My children and I traveled back to Virginia. Our energy shifted when we got closer to Ari's house. My stomach began to knot up and my chest would get tight. Being in that household was beginning to cause anxiety in me and my children. When we walked into Ari's home, you could tell that a conversation was being had about us because there was an awkward silence when we entered the room. I said, "Hello everyone!" Ms.

C replied, "Hello!" Ari didn't open her mouth and walked away as if she didn't see us standing there. It wasn't the first time that Ari didn't speak. There were many days when Ari would come home and I or my children would speak to her and she would completely ignore us. Ari was very childish and liked a lot of attention and she wanted people to kiss her butt, which was not something that I do. I refused to allow my children to kiss her butt as well.

My daughter KaRyzma looked up to Ari and she would always want to be around her, but Air would shun her. This made me angry and I was becoming very uncomfortable which made me very eager for my situation to change. I couldn't see myself staying in that house much longer. So I would apply to more jobs and go into places to get applications. I found out Burlington was hiring, and I applied for the cashier position. I wasn't too prideful to work as a cashier, I just needed something to get me out of what I was in.

I got called in for an interview to work at Burlington. I informed Ms. C and asked if she could watch Kelaiah for me during the interview. Ms. C congratulated and acted if she was happy for me, but I could hear the content in her voice. Ms. C stated that she would watch Kelaiah for me, but she wanted to go with me to the mall. I looked at her with astonishment and asked, "Why?" Ms. C stated that she wanted to get out of the house, and she was going to take Kelaiah to the play area in the mall.

I took Ms. C and Kelaiah with me to the mall and went to my interview. The interview went great and I got the job. I was so happy because it was a step closer to my goals. I informed Ms. C and she stated that she was happy for me. Then Ms. C stated, "I think I'm going to get a job with you." I asked, "Why?" Ms. C replied, "I'm ready to work now."

Ms. C would share her dreams with me, and I shared some of mine with her. Once I picked up on her jealous spirit, I stopped sharing with her my dreams. Ms. C was feeling a little intimidated because I was making moves towards my goals and she wasn't doing anything. I've always been a doer, not just a talker. If I say I am going to do something, eventually I will do it.

It was my first day at work, I went to complete all my initial paperwork and trainings. Ms. C watched Kelaiah for me. I would pray for Kelaiah every time I left her with Ms. C because I was becoming a little leery of her. I prayed that God would protect her and keep her safe and get us out of that house soon. I was scheduled to work the next day, which would have been my official first day on the register. I worked my hours and I paid Ms. C for watching Kelaiah. I was scheduled to work the next day. Later that night, I received a text from Ms. C that she couldn't watch Kelaiah for me while I worked tomorrow. Ms. C stated that she needed to go with Ari to handle some business. I began to laugh to myself. I knew that Ms. C was allowing her jealousy to override her decision in watching Kelaiah.

I contacted my supervisor to let her know that I wouldn't be able to come in the next day due to not having childcare. I was upset because it made me look bad and as if I was not dependable. I didn't want to put Kelaiah in daycare because it was so expensive. The next day Ari took off from work and Ms. C decided not to go with her. Ms. C stated, "I guess I could have watched Kelaiah after all." I was so mad because I felt like she was trying to sabotage my job. Ms. C was allowing her jealousy of me moving forward get the best of her. Ms. C spent most of her days in the home talking about her dreams and the things that she wanted to do. I was making steps towards my goals and aspirations. My steps may have been "baby steps" but at least, I was moving forward. When Ari returned, she had a brand-new car that looked identical to mine with the same color and all.

Ms. C started bragging on Ari's car and how she got it. I looked at her shaking my head while asking myself, "So this is why you couldn't watch my daughter while I went to work?" It was confirmed now that they were in competition with me. I couldn't understand it at all because I was a single mother and struggling just to get my family a place to stay and they were intimidated by little old me?

God reminded me that the enemy can see your future and potential even when you can't. God also reminded me that during those months that I had been staying there that we never had to ask them for money and He always provided for us. Even Ms. C brought it up to me and she couldn't understand how I wasn't working but never needed anything from them, other than a place to stay. I would tell Ms. C that it was all God and not my doing.

One Saturday, I received an email from Chuck who was the State Director of a Foster Care agency that I has previously applied to. He informed me that he reviewed my resume and application and invited me in for an interview. I attended the interview and got the job. It was about 3 weeks before I started working. My first day was March 18th, 2019. I was so happy, and I asked Ms. C would she babysit Kelaiah until I got her into a daycare? Ms. C agreed to watch her, but I knew that she it wouldn't last very long. Ms. C babysat Kelaiah for me the first week of my employment.

We went back to North Carolina to visit Kemarri for the second family day and he vented a lot. Kemarri stated that he was going through a lot in the school and that he was getting bullied and threatened daily. He informed me that some of the children there were court ordered to be there, so they didn't care about getting their education. So those children would make it miserable for all the other students there. That made me feel very uneasy because I am a very overprotective mother and I feel it was my job to keep my family safe. Before I left Kemarri, I spoke to one of the officers and asked him to look out for my son. The officer responded, "Your son needs to look out for himself." That didn't sit well with my spirit and I asked my son if he still wanted to continue his journey. Kemarri stated that he wanted to stay and that he would call me the next day to let me know how the rest of his day went.

We arrived back to Ari's house that next day. As time passed, I could feel more tension in the home. One-night Ari blew up in a tantrum and I asked what was wrong? She stated that my son was in the bathroom and was taking a long time on purpose. I responded, "What's really the issue here, because that's not a reason to blow up the way that you did?" Ms. C sent me a long text trying to excuse Ari for her behaviors. I went to Ms. C's room to address it because I was not going to argue with her over texts. I explained to Ms. C that I was a grown woman and respect goes both ways. I told her that Ari played a lot of games and was very rude to me and my children since we moved in. I also encouraged Ms. C to stop encouraging Ari's behaviors by not holding her accountable for her actions. Ms. C wasn't going to address the issues with Ari, because she didn't want Ari to argue with her or Ari put her out of her home. But I was at my wits end.

I SUPPORT HER

Ms. C contacted me to inform me that Ari's move date had been moved up and I needed to find someone else to watch Kelaiah and we needed to find somewhere else to stay. I laughed on the phone because I knew that she was not telling the truth. Although I laughed on the phone, this really infuriated me. If it was just me in this situation, I would have been able to brush it off. But Ms. C and Ari was hurting my children as well. Ms. C was mad that I was able to find a great job with benefits and things were moving along for my family. I contacted my sister and informed her of what was going on. My sister and her husband called my phone and offered to let us stay at their home until we were able to get our own. I was a little hesitant to move in with my sister because there have been some issues in the past with me and my brother-in-law and I didn't want any problems while we were in their home.

The next day, my children were having a difficult time completing their homework as it seemed that the internet was not working. I attempted to get the internet to work and informed Ari that the internet was down. Ari responded, "No it works just fine. I changed my password so that you or your children couldn't use it." I already knew Ari was childish, but to be that immature and petty to my children as well, was sad. Later that night, Kemarri called and I asked him how was he doing? Kemarri asked, "Mom, please come get me! I hate it here." I responded, "Don't worry, we are leaving here tomorrow and I will come get you right after we move out of here.

I talked with my children and told them that we needed to leave in the morning. My son and daughter agreed to stay home from school. The next morning, I got up very early to pick my sister up so that she could drive my car while I got a U Haul for our belongings. My sister lived and hour and 15 minutes away from where we had been staying. On the way to my sister's home, I missed the merge right sign and almost got into an accident with an 18-wheeler truck. Instead of hitting the truck, I decided to hit the orange and white barrel cones and my left side mirror popped off. At that moment, I wasn't concerned about the mirror because I almost lost my life.

I picked my sister up and picked up a U-Haul truck. My sister waited for me at my storage unit while I got our things and my children. While moving our stuff to the truck, my son said that he heard Ms. C laughing and saying, "Thank you, Lord for getting them out of here!" This angered me, but I had been trying not to react or respond to their pettiness the entire time that we lived with them. I was anxious, and I could feel my blood boiling. I knew that if she said anything to me, I was going react in a negative way. We were moving the last few items that we had left, and I guess we weren't moving fast enough for Ms. C. She decided to grab some of our things and take them outside. I immediately said, "No, I got it!" Ms. C responded, "No, I don't mind." I said, "No, please don't touch my stuff, I will move it." Ms. C said, "Well I was just trying to help you." I couldn't hold my tongue any longer and I blurted out, "No you were not trying to help me or my children. You both have done nothing but bullied my children and try to sabotage our progress. Thank you for opening up your home, but no thank you on how we were treated while we were here." I checked the room to ensure that it was clean, gave Ms. C my house key back and left.

We grabbed Kemarri's clothes from storage and drove to my sister's home. My sister stated that we could live in her basement until we got our own place. My son, Khyleed and I unpacked all the items out of the U-Haul and dropped the U-Haul off to a local U-Haul store. My children and I left to go to North Carolina to pick Kemarri up. I called the school to inform them that I was coming and why I was coming. I informed them that I was coming all the way to North Carolina to get my son and I wasn't leaving without him. I arrived at the school and signed the paperwork for them to release Kemarri to me. Kemarri's teacher tried to talk me out of taking him but I refused to listen. All I thought about was if I left him there and something happened to him, I would've never been able to forgive myself.

On our way to my sister's home I could tell Kemarri was having regrets of leaving the school. His became very quiet and sad like. When we arrived Kemarri greeted everyone and kind of stayed to himself. My sister said, "That is not the same boy that you dropped off to military school, is it?" I responded, "No, it's not! I need to figure out what's next for him." Later that night, I went to talk to Kemarri in the living room. I could tell that he had a lot on his mind. Kemarri began to panic and started slumping over to the ground, crying. He said, "Ma, I think I messed up. I shouldn't have left school. Now what am I going to do? My life is over now!" He just sobbed, lying on the ground. I picked his head up and held him in my arms and began to encourage him. I reminded him that God would not leave, nor forsake him. I said you may not have received your diploma that way, but we will find another way for you to get it. I told him don't worry about what everyone is going to think. Let them think what they want. When you are ready to pursue your education, you will. Kemarri stated that he wanted to get his high school diploma and not his GED. I reminded him that he would have to be focused and try his best so that he could obtain his goal

The next day, I enrolled KaRyzma into her third school for the year. She wanted to go to school with her little cousin. I was a little worried because I didn't want KaRyzma to fall behind in her work because we moved around so much. Kelaiah still couldn't attend school yet. I went to back to work and thanked my supervisor for giving me the day off so that we could move and pick my son up. My supervisor stated that it was fine. I felt so blessed that I finally had a job that I loved, and the people seemed to be nice. I worked hard every day to ensure that I applied what I was being taught. I was a Treatment Foster Care Case Manager for a Foster Care Agency. I drove an hour and 15 minutes to and from work each day for 6 months. My son didn't want to switch schools to my sister's county, so I kept him at the same school. I would get up at 5:45am to take him to school by 7:30am. I would sit at a restaurant across from my job for an hour and 30 minutes until I had to work at 9am. Work was great, and I was learning so much from my supervisor.

I did the same routine most days, worked Monday through Friday and cleaned up our area and the common area. I cooked about 3-4 times each week. My sister and I made a deal that I would pay her rent and help with food. Most Sunday's, I attended church in Woodbridge which was where my job was located as well. My children and I became very fond of Woodbridge and wanted to get a place there because it was closer to my job and the church that I was attending. Most of the time, my children and I stayed to ourselves because we didn't want to get in the way of my sister and her family's regular routine of life. I knew that my sister was married, and I always wanted to give them the space that they needed. My sister was pregnant, and I didn't want to add any more stress to her that she was already carrying. So, my children and I tried to help as much as we could. There were times when my brother-in-law would become upset and I would just encourage my children to stay out of it and mind their own business. I would always remind them that we were only going to be there for a moment and that we would have our own place very soon.

I didn't call my parents to tell them about the things that we were going through because I'm an adult, and I didn't want them to feel that they needed to save us. I didn't want anyone to suggest that me and my children return to North Carolina. I was determined not to return to North Carolina to live, only to visit.

Summer was here, and school was out. Months had passed, and I continued to follow the same routine of working during the week and church on the weekends. But as time went on, tensions began to rise throughout the house. I saw it coming but I tried to avoid it because I wanted to maintain peace within the home and family. There were times when my brother-in-law would come home from work upset, he would take it out on me or my children. I tried to deal with it as much as possible and tried not to take it personally. I knew that with a new baby coming, there were bound to be some stressful moments. My children and I would clean the house very frequently.

I knew that my sister couldn't do too much because she was very pregnant at this point. I cooked most nights after coming home from work. I would get frustrated when I got home to cook and realized that no one had cleaned the kitchen from their usage. If my brother-in-law cooked, he would leave the mess for me to clean. Which was fine, but I wasn't receiving the same courtesy. I had to clean up from previous nights before, cook and clean up after I cooked. All doing this after working an 8-hour shift and driving home for an hour and a half to get to the house. Although they let us live in their home, I was starting to feel unappreciated in a sense.

There were times where I would be at work and the children were at home and my sister would become upset with my 3-year-old and say, "Kelaiah, take your fucking ass to the basement." It was if my sister was referring to the basement as a place of lower value where me and children belonged. There were times where my children and I were not allowed on the top floor unless we were getting our shower. Anyone that knows me, knows that my children are my heart. I can take anything that people throw my way. But when you mess with my children, you are messing with me. When I would come to the house, my sister would act like nothing was ever said. I was beginning to realize that although we were invited in their home, their hearts were not in the right place. Some people will mistreat you when they feel that you need them, and they are your only hope. I wasn't shocked to get that treatment from my brother-in-law, but I was bothered that my own sister was going along with the disrespect and treatment.

There were times when I had to restrain from spending time with my sister. She was pregnant at the time and I felt like she needed me but I wasn't allowed to because my brother-in-law would get jealous and not want me around. My sister and I had always had a close relationship when we were children. We always been there for one another. But there had been a wedge for the last few years of our relationship. When I was still in North Carolina, my sister would tell me that her husband would get mad if we talked on the phone for over an hour. He never wanted her to spend much time with me. I wanted to spend time with my sister while she was pregnant but I knew that I couldn't get too close because her husband would get mad.

One night I went upstairs to my sister's room and we talked for hours about the baby and life. I was finally able to get comfortable with her again and I was giving her advice on items to get for the baby. I saw that she hadn't quite organized all of the baby's clothes, so I went to the store and purchased storage crate for the baby. I got back to the house and began to organize the baby's clothes and shoes. My brother-in-law became upset and started arguing with my sister. When my sister informed me that he was upset about me purchasing items for his child, I began to keep my distance from my sister. My oldest son told me that it probably wouldn't be a good idea to go to the hospital when my sister delivered the baby. I asked Kemarri, "Why not?" Kemarri responded, "He's already said that he's not letting anyone in the delivery room with Auntie." It would only be him and my niece.

So, I didn't take off from work when my sister was going to be induced because I didn't want to have a confrontation with my brother-in-law while my sister was in labor. It hurt me because my sister and I used to be so close and now she was allowing someone to come in between our relationship as sisters. I wanted to be there for her but I felt like I couldn't be.

Due to the tension that was in the home, it caused more tension between me and my children as well. There was a time where my son Kemarri and I were not speaking to each other for at least a month. He wanted to go back to North Carolina to visit with his family. I didn't mind him spending time with his family, but I didn't trust Kemarri's motives and reasons of wanting to go back. I didn't want him to go back and get with the wrong crowd and get into trouble. One day one of his older cousin's contacted me and asked if the boys could spend a week with him.

I told him that it would be okay for them to get away for a while. I didn't mind Kemarri going to North Carolina if his brother was going as well. I just didn't trust Kemarri. But unbeknownst to me, Kemarri manipulated Khyleed into not going to North Carolina. Kemarri knew that Khyleed was afraid of dogs and he stated that he's cousin's dog had been biting lately.

Kemarri came back from North Carolina and started back playing the game all day and sleeping. After a while, Kemarri became very bored and eventually became depressed. He needed something constructive to do, so I took him to a pizza delivery place to apply for a job. Kemarri worked the job for almost a month and it made him feel independent by making his own money. However, Kemarri did not stay to the job very long because he soon lost sight of why he was there.

By Kemarri not working anymore, he had too much idle time on his hands. Khyleed was still angry with Kemarri for manipulating him not to go to North Carolina to see his family. Kemarri was holding anger in from when he was at military school. Every other day there was an issue between Kemarri and Khyleed and it would escalate into an argument. One day, I was driving to my sister's house from work and I called Kemarri to see what they wanted for dinner because I didn't feel like cooking. Everything seemed to be okay when we were on the phone, so I told him that I would be there after I picked up dinner. About 5 minutes later, my sister called my phone yelling, "Kemarri and Khyleed are in here fighting and trying to kill each other. They are in here breaking all of my shit." I hurried to my sister's home and tried to stay as calm as possible. I didn't want to spike my blood pressure. My sister stated that my daughter ran to the neighbor's house and asked someone to help her break up the fight.

I SUPPORT HER

I arrived at the house and I noticed my sister and the neighbors were standing outside. As I walked in the house, I apologized to my sister for my boys disrespecting her home. It was a rough time in our lives, not having our own place to call home. It was beginning to take a toll on our relationships with each other. I walked in and found the boys in separate rooms. Kemarri was still upset and still wanting to fight. Khyleed was sitting calmly in the living room and I asked him what happened. He told me that it started after an exchange of words between the two of them. Khyleed stated that Kemarri headed towards him and they began to fight. I discussed how important it was to handle things in a calm manner and how to have each other's back instead of stabbing each other in it. I reminded them that they were brothers and that nothing and no one should separate them from each other. I said, "You both have been harboring anger in your hearts for quite some time now. Whatever the real issue is, let's talk about it."

My boys process things a little differently from me and they just avoided each other for a few weeks. Kemarri and Khyleed usually don't talk about their feelings but will show you their heart through their actions. One day, I took Kemarri with me to get some groceries from the store and Kemarri decided to buy some snacks for everyone. Kemarri stated that he was going to buy Khyleed's favorite snack. I turned and looked at him to see if he was serious and Kemarri had a straight face. I was so happy to see that his heart was not totally hardened for his brother. Khyleed had been frustrated about moving to a new place and going to new school and Kemarri was frustrated about what he endured in military school and that he left so prematurely, and they took their frustrations out on each other.

I SUPPORT HER

It was fall and school was back in session. I enrolled Kelaiah in a Pre-Kindergarten program and she was so excited. Kelaiah wanted to go to school because she wanted to be a big girl like her sister. My sister or niece would take the girls to school for me every day. I was very grateful that they were willing to transport the girls to school and pick them up daily. I was still so appreciative of them allowing us to stay in their home. My brother-in-law would come home nights and complain to my son asking why I didn't clean up the kitchen after he cooked the night before for his family. I told my son; I was getting tired of cleaning up his mess. One Friday night, I decided to clean the house and my children helped me. I usually would do a thorough cleaning most Saturday mornings, but I wanted to get the cleaning out of the way. I had a feeling that my brother-in-law was going to start complaining again and I wanted to avoid any conflict with him. I never wanted to give him any reason to try to kick us out of his home. The children and I scrubbed the kitchen, bathrooms, living room and the basement.

The next morning, we got up early to go to the laundromat. I went on the mid floor to the bathroom to go brush my teeth. I heard footsteps coming downstairs and my brother-in-law fussing to himself. I thought to myself, "Here we go again!" I knew that he was going to try to start an argument. I stayed in the bathroom waiting for him to leave. When I thought the coast was clear, I opened the door to leave. He came around the corner and said, "Kenesa, I want to talk to you." I froze like a child who had been caught sneaking in the house and my heart dropped. I turned around and said, "Okay, what about?" My brother-in-law said, "I need this house cleaned." I looked at him confused, as I had just cleaned the house the night before. "I need it spotless because my homeboy from work may be coming over today or tomorrow to spend the night." I replied, "I already cleaned the house last night. So, it's done." My brother-in-law interrupted while raising his voice, "Let me finish!" After that I began to tune him out. I knew he was looking for an argument or some type of conflict and I wasn't going to give it to him. After he was done, I said, "Okay!" and walked away.

I went to the basement and told my children that we needed to gather out laundry and go. I decided to get out of the house for the day, so we left. I texted my sister informing her of what her husband said and let her know that I didn't say anything to him out of respect for her. I told her that we were going to do laundry in Woodbridge and just spend the rest of the day there to give them some space. I get it, it was a lot of people in their home and we were bound to get on each other's nerves after a while.

We went to Woodbridge and I took the boys to get haircuts before we went to the laundromat. I received a call from my brother-in-law and I just let it ring. I did not want to run my blood pressure up by arguing with him because I knew that's what he wanted to do. He called my phone again and I told the kids that I was going to put him on speaker phone so that they could hear the conversation. I told my children that if he started any drama that I was going to end the call. I answered the phone and my brother-in-law asked, "What's wrong?" I responded, "I don't know. You tell me what's wrong with you." He said, "Your sister told me that you were upset about what I said to you." I responded, "You wouldn't even give me a chance to speak. I was trying to tell you that I cleaned the house last night. I could tell you had an attitude already this morning because you came downstairs fussing to yourself." My brother-in-law began to yell, "Kenesa, let me talk." I continued to explain to him why I got upset and he yelled louder, "Shut up and let me talk!" I ended the call. The next few days I tried my best to avoid seeing my brother-in-law. I wanted to be at peace, but I knew that we needed to get out of their house as soon as possible before another explosion occurred.

I began to look for homes in Woodbridge every week and I applied to 3 different apartments. I got denial letter from all 3 apartments. I was getting so frustrated and was becoming desperate. At work I met one of our new Foster Mothers, Ms. B, and we instantly clicked. Ms. B seemed to be a very humble and sweet person. One day we had to go on a visit to see a possible foster child for Ms. B and we talked about our families and life experiences. Ms. B. was so knowledgeable as she had been in the military and traveled the world.

I thought that I could learn a lot from Ms. B, and she seemed so eager to share some tips with me about investments and housing resources. Ms. B shared a lot with me about her children and family which made me feel more comfortable around her and able to let my guard down. I began to share with her some of my experiences with my family and what we were currently going through at the time. I told her that we were trying to get our own place and I was working hard on getting my bills caught up and credit score up. Ms. B seemed so concerned and acted as if she cared about what we were going through. Ms. B informed me that she had a 5-bedroom home that she shared with her daughter and grandson. Ms. B informed me that she had 2 daughters but the one that lived in her home, she couldn't stand. Ms. B went on and on telling me that her daughter had been living with her several years and would not help her pay any bills in the home.

Ms. B stated that she wanted her daughter out of her home and that if she didn't start helping her soon, that she was going to ask her to leave. I really felt for Ms. B, as she appeared to be going through a tough time in her home with her daughter and I couldn't understand how her daughter could treat her so bad. At the end of the visit Ms. B invited me and my children to her home for dinner one day. I said, "Ms. B, I can't do that because I could lose my job." Ms. B replied, "It will be okay you can come over and we can discuss my potential foster child and I can help you get a government job with more benefits for you and your family." Ms. B stated that she still had some connections in the government, and she could get me a job that paid double of what I was making. I liked my job, but I felt that I needed more money to get a home that I could afford. I went home and told my children about the nice new lady that I met and that she invited us over to her home.

Some time had passed, and Ms. B reached out to me and asked if I was coming over to her home. I was kind of hesitant because I didn't want to cross any boundaries by visiting her home without work being involved. About a month later, I was working in the office all day alone. I had opened the office and was going to be the person that closed the office that day because everyone else had either vacation time off or working at another office. Ms. B called and asked if she could drop some paperwork off to the office. I told her that it was fine and that I would be expecting her.

Ms. B showed up to the office with the papers and asked if I could make a copy for her. I agreed, and she begin to say that my children and I had been on her heart lately and that she really wanted to help us. I began to cry because I knew that things were not getting any easier at my sister's house. Ms. B asked, "Why don't you and your family come to my house for dinner on Sunday?" I responded, "We would love to!" "I will talk to the kids about it and let you know what time." I said. Ms. B asked, "Let me know what foods you and your children like, daughter," I smiled and said, "Aww that's so sweet! Thank you so much, you have made my day." I went home that evening and told my children about the sweet lady who invited us to her home for Sunday dinner.

Sunday came, and the children and I went to church. After church I called Ms. B and asked her if it was okay to come over? Ms. B stated that it was okay and that she already started cooking. We went over to Ms. B home and it was beautiful. I was impressed and honored to be there. Ms. B invited us in and made us feel welcomed. Once inside, we met Ms. B's daughter, "Vee" and grandson, "X." Ms. B's daughter stated that her and her son made plans to go somewhere else for dinner, so they left. When Vee and X left, Ms. V began to talk about her daughter and stated that she would be glad when she moves out of her home. I couldn't understand why Ms. V would talk about her daughter like that because she seemed very nice. I could tell there was some intense history between them.

Ms. B finished cooking and we began to eat. Ms. B said, "God told me to help you and your family. So, if there is any way that I can help you and your family, don't hesitate to ask." I responded, "Okay I will keep that in mind." Ms. B turned to my oldest son Kemarri and said, "She didn't hear me, so I will say it to you. If there is anything that you need me to help you with, don't hesitate to ask." I replied, "Okay, we may need you now. I don't know if I can stay there much longer." My back was up against the wall and I didn't want any more conflict to take place at my sister's home, because I didn't want to ruin our relationship.

Ms. B agreed that we could stay with her for a while until we got our place. Ms. B even told me that she had a townhouse that she was renting out to a family and that if things didn't work out with them that she would allow me the rent the townhome. I was so happy because it looked as if everything was looking up for my family. We rented a U-Haul and parked it at Ms. B's house.

The next morning, I got up early to get the U-Haul. I parked my car at Ms. B's house and headed to my sister's home. The girls were taken to school by my niece, so the boys helped me move our things to the truck. It began to rain, and we tried to as quickly as possible to get everything out in a timely manner. Kemarri and Khyleed cleaned the basement after everything was in the truck. It took us about 40 minutes to get everything in the truck. As we were finishing up, I texted everyone in the house and thanked them for opening their home to my family.

My boys and I headed to Woodbridge to unpack our things. We were so happy to be moving closer to my job, Khyleed's school and our church. Woodbridge was the first place we moved to after we left North Carolina and we fell in love with the area. I was excited for Kemarri to experience it. He had been to Woodbridge many times with us when we went to church, but it would be his first time living there. We were moving in with Ms. B who was this little old sweet lady, what could possibly go wrong? Ms. B had a 3-story home and her daughter lived in the basement. So, my children and I moved into a room on the top floor. It was big enough for us to put two air mattresses and our belongings in the room. We made it work as we had been in the last two homes, we stayed in. Ms. B and I came up with an agreement on my rent payment. Ms. B said that it would cover all utilities and stay.

We moved in October 1st and I enrolled KaRyzma in an elementary school nearby. KaRyzma was able to ride the bus which was convenient. When completed KaRyzma's paperwork, I informed the school that my family was homeless and that we were living with someone else's home. The school informed me that my family eligible for a program that helped homeless people with transportation for children in school and assist with resources. I went to several schools trying to get Kelaiah enrolled but every school stated that she had to live in the district.

I called several times for about a month trying to reach someone to help me get Kelaiah in school. Kelaiah would cry every morning because she wanted to go to school like her older brother and sister. Kemarri would stay home and babysit Kelaiah for me, while I worked. After a while Kemarri began to get bored and depressed again. I knew that he needed something to do other than babysitting, but I didn't want to put Kelaiah in daycare.

We had been living in the home for a few weeks and it was peaceful for the most part. Ms. B gave me a house key and she was being sweet. It was like we had a new family. She let me know that she had a security system and gave me a fob along with my new house key. Ms. B also informed me that she had a camera in her home. She said that the camera was to keep her and her family safe, not to spy on anyone. Ms. B would help KaRyzma with her homework and play board games with them. Ms. B had many rules in her home such as don't touch the walls, don't walk upstairs with your shoes on, clean up behind yourself, and make yourselves at home. Ms. B would constantly ask if we were okay because we stayed in the room most of time we were in the house. I told her that we were just trying to stay out of her way and didn't want to get on her nerves. I previously shared with her what we endured at Ms. C and

I SUPPORT HER

my sister's home. Ms. B would say, "I don't know how people could just be so mean to people."

I was so grateful to be staying at Ms. B's home and she continued to say that she could help us, and she wanted to teach me so many things. Ms. B talked about her daughter a lot when we were in the home and I would listen and try to encourage her to talk to her. Ms. B stated that her older daughter use to stay with her too, but she married a bum and moved out into their own home. Ms. B stated that she didn't like her older daughter's husband because he was disrespectful. She said, "My daughter's husband is trifling and make all that money and don't know what to do with it. One day he got into an argument and he cursed me out on my home and that bitch didn't say anything to defend me." I asked shockingly, "Who are you talking about?" Ms. B responded, "My daughter! Both are bitches." I was speechless and I could believe that she was talking about her daughters like that. I wondered where all that pain stemmed because Vee seemed like a nice person. She treated me and my children with the upmost respect and we were getting along fine.

I decided to cook dinner for everyone because Ms. B stated that she was so tired. Ms. B was retired, and she would pick up one of the elders from her church about once a week to take her shopping. I began to prep my food and Ms. B came in the kitchen. We began to talk about the day as I started cooking. Ms. B got up and started taking over my meal that I was preparing for everyone. I didn't mind the help, but I agreed to make dinner for everyone because she stated that she was so tired. I just brushed it off and kept cooking.

While we were eating, Ms. B began to give us a speech about how to use paper towels, napkins, toilet tissue and Kleenex. Ms. B stated that she had been watching how we used the them and that we were using them all wrong. I informed Ms. B that tissue and Kleenex could be used for the same purpose as well as napkins and paper towels. Ms. B stated that the children should not use the paper towels because they were wasteful. I responded, "Ms. B, I am the one that's been buying the paper towels since I've been here. It's not that big of a deal." I would buy dish-detergent, trash bags, paper plates, plastic cups, laundry detergent, tissue and paper towels for the house, so I couldn't understand why it bothered her how the children used it. I started noticing that I was having to buy more of those items sooner than before. One day I went to the basement to do some laundry and found all the items that I bought hidden behind the refrigerator.

The boys became big brothers to Ms. B's grandson, and they would sit up all night playing video games on the weekend. Ms. B would get upset if her daughter would leave the house and not tell her where she was going. One night, Ms. B's older daughter came to the house and brought her children. They seemed to be nice people, but I was leery of them because if all the things that Ms. B told me about them. When they would come over, I would stay upstairs in the room to give them some family time. Ms. B would always say, "My older daughter doesn't come to see me. She only started coming back over here because you all are here."

Kemarri would wash our clothes for us every week while we were at work and school but other than babysitting his sister, he had too much idle time. I wanted Kemarri to either enroll back in school or get a job. I was determined to get Kelaiah in school. I asked my co-worker who I should I call to get Kelaiah in Pre-Kindergarten. My co-worker used to be a schoolteacher for the county so I knew that she would know who to call. 10 minutes later, my co-worker emailed me the contact information of the director of the Pre-kindergarten program. I contacted the director and was able to complete the application and get her medical records to the director. There were so many children in the county so children could only attend the class for a half a day. I asked if Kelaiah could attend the morning class. Since we were in the Homelessness program, the school was able to bus Kelaiah to and from a school out of our district. Kelaiah was so happy, she was finally back in school.

Ms. B's daughter decided that she was moving to Ohio and she informed Ms. B only a few days before she left. This made Ms. B upset which was shocking to me because she talked so much about wanting to kick her out of her home. I realized Ms. B was only speaking out of anger, but she really didn't want her daughter to leave at all. Ms. B's daughter moved to Ohio and we promised her that we would help keep an eye on her son for her. Ms. B went in her room and shut the door. Ms. B stayed in the room and no one saw her for 3 days straight. I knew she must have been upset for her to shut down like that.

After the 3rd day, Ms. B came out of her room as if nothing happened. We were still living as a family, but the atmosphere had certainly changed. Ms. B became very bitter and angry a lot. She would constantly complain about every little thing every day. Suddenly, the things that we regularly did in the home became a problem for Ms. B. She complained about how where I hung the dish towel, marks on the wall, marks on the stairs carpet, couldn't use the ice maker, couldn't use the stove, couldn't watch television in the living room, no one could sit in her den area, couldn't take long showers, couldn't take showers after midnight, and couldn't wash clothes on the weekend because it would run the bill up. The list goes on and on. Everything that we did, Ms. B had a problem with it.

I was very uncomfortable, and my children were feeling as if there were in a prison. My children and I would have conversations while driving in the community and Ms. B would literally say the exact same thing that we were talking about. When I first met Ms. B, I thought this lady is spiritual and she can read my thoughts. But after a while, the "weird coincidences" became very frequent. The children and I were talking while going to church and KaRyzma said, "Ma, Ms. B has a lot of wine bottles in the house. She must drink a lot." I laughed and responded, "Yeah, she should probably put it out of reach of children."

Later that day, Ms. B and I were talking in the kitchen and she said, "Yes I do have a lot of wine in my house. I have it here for when I have company over or a family gathering." I paused shockingly because I was trying to figure out where that came from. One day I picked Khyleed up from school and I asked, "What do you want for dinner tonight?" He responded, "I wouldn't mind having some of your homemade burgers." I said, "I haven't made that in a while. Okay, I will make try to make sometime this week. I took him back to my job with me to finish up my workday. When we got to the house, Ms. B said, "Good evening! Dinner's ready!" I said, Awesome, what are we having?" Ms. B put the food on the table and said, "Burgers!" I looked at Khyleed and he looked at me at the same time, as if we were thinking the same thing.

Later that night, I brought up what happened before dinner to my children. I said, "Is it me or am I tripping? Why do I feel that Ms. B is listening to our conversations?" Kemarri responded, "No, I don't think so.

You're tripping mom. That lady wouldn't do that." I said, "No, Son, I am being serious right now! It has been too many instances where we talk about something when we are not around her and she knows our conversation." Kemarri said, "I'm sorry, Ma. But I just can't believe that she would do something like that." I responded, "Okay!" But I wasn't convinced that she wasn't listening. I became so paranoid when talking with my kids. I always felt like she was watching or listening.

As time progressed, so did the tension in the home. I began to see more controlling behaviors from Ms. B. She started complaining more and more about the kids. One day she wanted to have a talk with me. So, I went downstairs to talk to Ms. B and she spoke so badly about my children and how they didn't put things the way that she wanted them to be. I apologized to her for all informed her that my children weren't perfect and that even I was going to make mistakes and not get it right. I reminded her that we were human and may not get all her rules the way that she wanted but that we were trying. Ms. B was showing some obsessive-compulsive behaviors. I was beginning to realize that she wasn't wrapped too tight in the head.

I went upstairs and talked with my children about the things that Ms. B was complaining about. I asked them to do whatever she asked just so we didn't have any conflict with her. I asked them to respect Ms. B in her home and not to be rude to her just because she was being petty. Kemarri became upset because he was fond of Ms. B and couldn't understand why she had complaints about him. So Kemarri stopped talking to Ms. B and he even stopped speaking to her grandson. His feelings were hurt by the things that she said about him. I reminded Kemarri, "Do you still think that she is the same little sweet lady that we first met?" Kemarri responded, "Not at all."

While I was at work and the children were at school, Kemarri and Ms. B were the only two in the home. Kemarri would go downstairs to eat or wash clothes and would not say anything to Ms. B. This made Ms. B terribly upset that Kemarri was ignoring her. That evening when I came home, Ms. B called another meeting with me. This time she stressed how disrespectful Kemarri was for not speaking to her all day in the home. I spoke to Kemarri about his behaviors and demanded that he apologize to Ms. B. Kemarri apologized and began to speak to Ms. B but he still would not engage in a conversation with her anymore because he was still hurt by what she said.

Ms. B continued to complain about my children and what they were doing or not doing. She stated that Kemarri should get a job and stop sitting in the house all day. I responded, "Kemarri does not have a job because I need him to help me with Kelaiah." Kemarri was in the kitchen one day and he knew where the camera was in the house. So, he stuck his middle finger up at the camera. Ms. B saw Kemarri in the camera and texted me that she wanted to talk to me about something. I asked the children, "What did you all do now?" Kemarri asked, "What are you talking about?" I responded, "Ms. B just asked to speak to me again. Kemarri began to tell me about what he did and explained why he did it.

I was so angry with him, and made him apologize to Ms. B. I said to Kemarri, "Since you have too much time on your hands, I'm going to take you to apply for a job." I drove to a nearby pizza delivery place and urged him to speak to the manager about employment. Kemarri hesitantly went inside to speak to the manager. While inside, Kemarri asked the manager for an application and told her that he needed a job. The manager basically hired Kemarri on the spot and told him to complete the paperwork and bring his identification cards back to her along with the application. Kemarri became very fond of his job and the people he worked with.

I knew that I had to get out of there soon, it was like the walls were closing in on me. I knew that I was not supposed to be living in her home because I was a Treatment Foster Care Case Manager and Ms. B was a Foster mother. I was breaking boundaries by living in her home, but I did not know where else to go. So, I began my house hunt again and I was given the name of a Housing Agent to help me look for a home of our own. I met with the Agent on a Saturday and she told me what I needed to do to get my credit score up so that I could buy a home. I took the information that she had given me and knew that I had a lot of work ahead of me.

One day Ms. B was waiting for us to come to the house, and she wanted to talk again to complain about the children and her concerns. The more she complained about, the more I just stood there looking at her. I was determined not to give Ms. B the reaction that she was looking for. Ms. B continued to complain, and I still would not react. Ms. B decided to turn the conversation up a notch and say that she believed that Kemarri was violent and that she was afraid for her safety. At this point, I knew how mentally unstable Ms. B was, and I was not going to continue to subject my children and I to her ridiculous allegations of any sort. I was even more determined to get out of Ms. B's home.

I received a call from the Case Manager, Meg of the Homelessness program one day. She called to check on me and my children and to see if we needed help with anything or any linkage to resources. I told her that the only thing we needed was assistance with finding a home to call our own. Meg asked if we felt safe where we were. I told her that I was beginning to feel extremely uncomfortable because I knew that Ms. B was becoming more anal about things not being a certain way in the home. I knew that Ms. B could ask us to leave her home any given day and I wanted to be one step ahead of her. Meg told me about transitional housing and sent me the application. I completed the application and was feeling a little more secure that I was making moves that was getting us closer to our home.

Although Ms. B stated that she wanted me to rent her townhome from her, I was beginning to think that it was a bad idea. I did not want to make any business deals with Ms. B because I witnessed some shady business from her, and I did not want to get involved anything shady. Ms. B was telling me that she was going to put her current tenant out so that she could move me in her townhome. That did not sit well with me because I knew that her tenant had children in the home. If she could be so casual about them, then why would I think that she would treat me and my family any better.

One night, Kemarri and I were quietly talking in the room and he stated, "Ma, do you know what I've been craving that I haven't had in a while?" I asked, "What's that?" "Homemade French toast." I responded, "Well I will make you some soon." The next morning Kemarri and I were sitting in my car warming it up before I took him to work. Ms. B pulled up in her truck and got out with some groceries. She rushed over to my car and I rolled down my window. Ms. B said, "Good morning, I went to the store this morning because I was going to make you breakfast. I stated,

"Aww, that's so sweet! I will be right back. I have to take Kemarri to work." Ms. B replied, "I'm making homemade French toast."

I turned to look at Kemarri with a sarcastic look on my face and said, "What a coincidence! We were just talking about that last night." Ms. B stated looking in the car at Kemarri, "I will make sure to put some aside for you." Kemarri responded, "Thank you, I appreciate that!" I rolled my window up as I drove away. I looked at Kemarri and asked, "Now do you believe that she is listening to our conversations?" Kemarri replied, "Oh my God, Mom! That lady's crazy!" I said, "Yep and she is listening to our conversations and watching us on videos at the house. Our privacy was being invaded, but we were living in her home and we felt that there was nothing we could do about.

Christmas was quickly approaching, and I didn't have the extra money to buy Christmas gifts for my children. I told them that I couldn't get them anything this year, which would have made 2 years in a row that they wouldn't have received any gifts. Meg called me and invited me to a "Free Christmas Shopping Spree" for the children. KaRyzma's school sent a letter home asking for the girls' sizes and what toys they wanted for Christmas. I also received another call from the school with the third opportunity to purchase gifts from Target. I began to cry because I was so excited and humbled.

The weight of keeping the secret that I was staying with Ms. B was weighing on me. So, I went my director to let him know what was going on. I was so sure that it was going to be my last day at the agency because I knew that I had a crossed a line. I explained to my director that I was desperate to have some where for my children and I to go and that I didn't want to sleep in my car. Surprisingly, my director was not upset and stated that he understood why I did it. He asked me to get out of Ms. B's home as soon as possible. I told him that I would. He asked to tell my co-workers what was going as well. I told my co-workers and told them what we were going through with Ms. B.

My supervisor invited my children and I to their home Christmas Eve. I took my children, and my supervisor and his family bought my children Christmas presents. I was so overjoyed to see my children's faces as they smiled. God had answered my prayers and I didn't have to pay anything for their gifts. The next week at work, I was venting to my co-workers about Ms. B's behaviors in the home. My son had told me that Ms. B had a secret passageway in her home, and she used that secret passageway to spy on us and listen to our conversations. My co-worker stated that she would pay for a weekend at a hotel so that we could get a break from Ms. B for a while. My supervisor said, "That's all nice and everything, but she needs to get out of there for good. I'm going to talk to my family and see if we can get the church to pay for a week in the hotel.

I was nervous because I was unsure of how Ms. B was going to react or how my children would feel about it. I went home and spoke to my children and they agreed that we needed to leave Ms. B's home as soon as possible. We packed a few outfits and left for the hotel. While we were at the hotel, my supervisor called and stated that his family was going to help us move our things out of Ms. B's home that Saturday. I became nervous because I didn't want there to be any conflict with Ms. B when we tried to move our things out.

We arrived at Ms. B's home on Saturday morning, January 4th, 2020 to move our things. I gave Ms. B the house key and security fob back. I thanked Ms. B for opening her home to my family and I and we moved our things out. I felt better that we no longer had to live up to unrealistic expectations. We were free finally from bondage and the evil little lady.

I thought it was nice that we had somewhere to stay for a week, but I knew that we couldn't stay there forever. So, I continued to call Meg to check on my application status at the transitional housing. My co-workers were helping me look online for basement apartments to rent. I was applying for 1-bedroom basement apartments that we would have to share with another family. I got a few calls back asking me to come take a look at the basements to see if I was still interested. 2 of them were okay but there was one that I really liked. It had many of the amenities that I was looking for, even though it was a 1 bedroom. I figured my children and I had lived in smaller spaces, so we could make it work for a while. I ended up getting denial after denial from all the basement apartments. I still had hope and was waiting to hear back from the transitional home.

My co-worker extended our stay at the hotel for another week. I was so grateful to have people in our lives who genuinely cared and was concerned for our safety. I would think about my situation and just shake my head with astonishment. I thought it was so ironic that I was a Treatment Foster Care Case Manager who helped to make sure that children were in safe and adequate homes and yet here I was a single mother and didn't have a home for my own children. That motivated me to keep the faith and to never give up on finding a home for my family. I continued to my search for a home and I was determined not to give up. I could not believe that God brought us this far just to leave us.

There were times when doubt would enter my mind, but God would constantly remind me that He was still able. I started thinking about my goals again and I wanted to accomplish this year. So, I wrote down my vision board for the year 2020. On that list was that I would become a Certified Life Coach. I would constantly check the school's website to map when I wanted to take the class. I saw that there was a class coming up January 17th- 19th and the next one was scheduled in May. I didn't want to wait until May because I didn't know where I would be or what would be doing by the time May came along. I waited so long for this opportunity that I didn't want to miss it. I had filed my taxes and was able to receive a loan on it. I caught up on a few of my bills and paid for my class in full.

I was so excited to attend the class and nervous as well. We had been living in a hotel now for a week and a half and I still had not been approved for a home yet. I didn't know what my future was going to look like or where we were going when we left the hotel. I had no concrete plan. My faith was in God and I had to completely trust Him with my whole heart. I extended my stay at the hotel for a few more days to cover the days that I would be in Washington D.C for my Life Coaching class. Not many people knew what my children and I were going through except for my co-worker's and my cousin. I always kept my cousin posted on our where abouts and movements.

I also knew that it was time to renew my car registration and I had to get a lot of work done on my car before I could get my inspection. My entire windshield was cracked, and my left side mirror had been broken for months. I contacted Safelite AutoGlass and scheduled for them to come and repair my windshield at the hotel the on Martin Luther King Day. I attended my class for the 3 days and my children stayed at the hotel in Dumfries. I would check on them on each break that I was given to make sure they were okay. I made sure they always had something there to eat. Each day the staff told us that we would have to pay for parking which was about $13 for the entire day. At the end of each day, I would get to the gate to pay for my parking and received favor each time. I never had to pay a dime for parking the entire weekend. That confirmed it for me and let me know that I was meant to be there. At my class, I met some nice people. I enjoyed hearing their stories and learning from them as we completed different workshops. Our instructor was amazing and taught us many techniques to implement when coaching and in life. At the end of the third day, we all received our certificates, graduated and ended it with a prayer.

The next morning, I got my windshield repaired. It was our last day at the hotel. So, we had to pack our things again and we were tired of moving. We were ready to be settled in our home. My supervisor and his family were trying to move us to an extended stay hotel which would have been doors from the hotel that we were staying in. But they were unable to reserve the extended stay. So, they moved just to the hotel next door with wasn't as nice, but it was cheaper. We moved our things into the room and the room was bigger than the room at the other hotel, but it was not clean. My boys and I used to work at the Outer Banks as cleaners and inspectors, and we were very particular about things being clean. My son Khyleed immediately went to the bathroom to inspect it. Khyleed stated that the bathroom was nasty. The bathroom sink and tub had hair in it and the floor was gritty. I even found a dried-up washcloth hanging up in the shower rod. We checked the sheets and found some hair on it. I called to the front desk and informed the manager that I was unhappy with the room. She apologized and told me to come downstairs to get a key to another room.

I went downstairs to get the key and decided to check the other room out. Khyleed and I went inside and as soon as we opened the door, a terrible stench hit us in the face. The room was just as nasty as the room that we were in. I went to work the next day and my supervisor asked me how I night went. I told him what happened and how uncomfortable we were the night before. My supervisor called his family and told them that we needed to get out of there. My supervisor's family, The Laws, discussed what they should do and decided to open their home to my family.

We were moving again. I was still searching for homes online and checking in with Meg to see where we were in the application process for the transitional home. Meg stated that were reviewing our application and would be giving us a call soon. I was scheduled to see another 1-bedroom basement apartment as well. I wanted to keep my options open. I went to see the basement apartment and it was very nice. Although it was not as big, I would have liked, we were going to make it work. I completed the application for it and called the realtor daily to check on the status of the application. About 5 days later, I called again to check to see if we got the apartment and the realtor denied us. He stated that my eviction showed up on my background and credit check. It seemed like the eviction was still haunting us. I paid the rental company in full so I couldn't understand why it was still holding me back.

I became frustrated and began to cry in my office. I contacted my sister and informed her of that I was applying for homes, but my eviction was hindering me from moving forward. I asked my sister what I should do. She told me the only way that they would remove the eviction off my background is if I paid my bill off. I informed her that it was paid, and she told me to contact all the credit bureaus and ask them to remove it from my report. I typed a letter and provided the letter stating that I didn't owe any more money for my old apartment.

I received a phone call from a Case Manager at the Transitional Home, and she asked me to come in for an interview. She began to give me a little information about the program and stated that, "This program is strict, and you would have a curfew and be limited on what you can spend per month." I was willing to do whatever it took for my children and I to have a home. When I arrived at the interview, I met with 3 women. 2 of them were Case Managers and one of them was a therapist. I could tell that one of the Case Managers was not open to giving me a chance at the program. She asked me my job title and I told her that I was a Case Manager like her. She told me that they would discuss it and get back to me.

I left and tried to be positive about it, but I didn't feel that the meeting went well, but I remained hopeful. A few days later, I received an email that I was denied for transitional housing. I was so disappointed, and I knew I had to keep trying. I didn't want to overstay our welcome with my supervisor and his family as I felt that I did with the others. At the Laws home, they made us feel at home. It was a good feeling not to have anyone tell you not to touch the wall or you could not wash your hands in the kitchen sink. The Laws treated us with the upmost respect and kindness, and they became family to us. My supervisor wanted me to transfer my children to the schools in their county, but I did not think that it was necessary. I would tell him, "I don't need to transfer my children's school because we are not going to be here that long." I was determined to have our own and I was not going to settle for anything other than that.

I contacted my realtor and informed her that I had applied to many rentals, and even the transitional home, and got denied. I explained to her my financial situation and told her that my eviction was hindering me with getting approved. She told that she would call around to see what was available. I told her that I was going to check some apartments on my own as well. That evening I left work and picked up my children, and I decided to get a few applications at some local neighborhoods. I immediately remembered driving by an apartment complex one day with the kids and they were advertising move in specials, so we decided to go there first. When we arrived, I went in the office and asked for an application. The Leasing Specialist was so nice and offered me some refreshments while she got me an application. She asked me to have a seat and when I was looking to move in. I told her that we needed to move in immediately. I began to tell her that we were homeless and that we were staying with my supervisor and his family.

The leasing manager asked if I wanted to see what the apartment looked like? I replied, "Yes, I would love to see it." My children and I followed her to the unit and walked in. It was beautiful with upgraded appliances, balcony and laundry room with a washer and dryer in the unit, 2 full bathrooms, free water, sewage, cable and internet. I explained to her that we moved from North Carolina and had been in Virginia for a little over a year and we were denied housing so many times. She was trying not to become emotional as she was listening to our experiences. As we were leaving, I asked her, "Would our apartment would look like this unit?" She responded, "This would be your unit." I was so happy and hopeful that we would get approved for the apartment.

We returned to the Law's home and I informed my supervisor that we were denied for the transitional home. He stated, "It's okay! You guys can stay here for as long as you want." Although I was appreciative of their patience and willingness to help, I was so eager to have our own place. I wanted that so much. It was nothing like having my own place to call home where I did not have to abide by no one's rules but your own. My oldest son and I completed the application and I turned them in the next morning.

The director at my job called a staff meeting to discuss progress and status with our cases. While in the meeting, I received a phone call. I excused myself, walked to my office and answered it. It was the Leasing Specialist from the apartment to let me know the status of my application. I braced myself for the worse. She said, "Ms. Bowe, I just wanted to let you know that you and your family have been approved for the unit." I paused and replied shockingly, "What did you say?" She repeated, "You and your family have been approved for the unit." I began to cry while thanking her and God!" I was so happy, and it was one of the best feelings that I had felt in a long time. My co-workers heard me crying and one of them came into the room to check on me.

I went back into the conference room and they asked me if I was okay. I informed them that we were approved for our apartment. My co-workers were shocked to hear that because they knew that we had received several denials in the last few weeks. My supervisor gathered some friends from his church to help move us in that following weekend. We moved into our new home on February 8th, 2020. It was a beautiful day and was very sentimental to me because the spiritual meaning of the number 8 is "New Beginnings."

When we started this journey, I knew that it was not going to be easy. I knew that we would face some trials and tribulations, but I just did not know what those tribulations were going to be. I prayed everyday asking God to guide us to the promise and He did just that. When God shows you the promise, He doesn't tell you what you will go through to get to the promise. But just know that when you get there, it will be worth it. Although we experienced some difficult times with others and within our own family, we learned some valuable lessons from each family and home. God taught us how to love and support each other. He taught us how to love others and have compassion for them when they are going through a difficult time. Being homeless humbled us and matured us in a way that we were not before. It taught us how to treat others and know when to be a blessing. It taught us how not to treat others when they are vulnerable and need our help. The year of 2019 gave us a greater understanding and meaning of our purpose.

Looking back at it all, I realized that God had taken us through different levels at each home. Every home that we lived in was bigger than the last one. We were able to see what the fruits of hard labor and what life could look like at each level. We were able to see how cold and lonely a home looks when you idolize money or things. We were able to see what a warm and loving home looks like when you put God and other people's needs first. There were times when my children questioned if God would deliver us out of bondage and I would encourage them and myself by reminding them that God did not bring us this far to leave us. I had to trust God with all my being. Moving back to North Carolina was not an option for me.

We are forever grateful for the experience because it helped to build us instead of breaking us. It made us stronger as individuals and as a family. We love harder and we support each other more. I thank God for the journey and for never leaving my family's side. The good, the bad and the ugly helped make us into the individuals that we are today. We are better people because of this experience. We are better people because we truly saw God's love for us through this experience.

Without God keeping me and my family through it all, we would have never made it. We would have given up and went back to North Carolina if I did not believe in God's promise to us. It has motivated me to continue to trust God and honor Him, because He will always come through. God always keeps His promises and He kept His promise to me, and my family and I will forever be grateful for it.

Our journey being homeless was different from what is depicted on television. We did not "appear" to be homeless or lacking at all. My oldest son and I continued to hold a job for most of the year. It was very difficult to save money because we had to pay bills and purchase food where we were living. On the outside looking in, we were doing fine. No one knew about our situation unless we told them, and we only shared it with a few people. Just because someone does not appear to be homeless, does not mean that they are not or that they don't need assistance. There are so many people in this world that are going through this, and are not getting the help that they need because they are afraid to speak up for many reasons.

Thank God, we had our faith to help get us through one of the toughest times that we ever had to endure. If your family or someone you know if going through a battle like ours or even worse, contact your local

"Homelessness Prevention Program" to get assistance. Contact a local homeless shelter and ask if there are any transitional housing that can assist you with a more permanent place to stay. If you have access to social media, there are several groups on Facebook that dedicate their time to assist homeless people with resources. Some of those groups are "Helping the Homeless Survive & Achieving a Place to Call Home," "National Faces of Homelessness," and "Helping our Homeless Ministries."

CHAPTER 4

Hidden Sentence

"No One Prepares You for Coming Home"

By: Pamela O'Hara

Here I am again. My name is Cooper. I am the one who has been traveling around the world with the B.O.P. Bureau of Prisons! They have just transferred me from Dublin, California, also known as Pleasanton FCI. They lost me in the system. Can you believe that? While I was in Oklahoma Detention Center, freezing my butt off. All because I refused to wear someone else's used panties. Two weeks after they found me here, I sat in R&D in Danbury FCI, along with the two girls that was on the van with me. I don't think I am going to like it here. Listen to me, as if I had a choice, talking about I don't like it here. Nobody cares if I like it here or not.

"Cooper?"

"Yeah."

"Come on, I got to take you the laundry."

We walked out of the R&D, I stopped…SNOW! And I continued to look around me. It wasn't much to see. I mean it is a compete circle.

"This is it? This is the compound?"

He laughed and said "Oh, it's bigger than it looks."

"Oh, for real? You could have fooled me!"

We went to laundry, where I got my bedding, uniforms, tee shirts, socks, underwear, boots, and a jacket. I put all the items in a laundry bag.

"You'll be in Unit 5," he said to me as we walked out the laundry area. He took me to my unit and gave me my cubicle number. I went to my cub and there, lying on her bed was, Tracy. I put my stuff on the chair and started making my bed, while Tracy stood there sizing me up. As I made my bed, I was thinking to myself… "Yeah, whatever you are thinking, just stop. You think long and you are going to think wrong. Please do not try me."

Tracy had got up and was just standing there, watching me. Finally, she said, "Hey you, what's your name?"

I stopped fixing my sheets and turned around and said "My name is Cooper, not hey you. What's yours?"

I SUPPORT HER

With an attitude, she said, "Look, all I asked was what's your name, let's not get off on the wrong foot here, okay? I mean, you are moving into my cub, so don't come in here all smart mouth and shit."

I just looked at this piece of nothing and said, "Lady, you don't know nothing about me, and I don't want to know nothing about you. I can promise you this, I won't be your roommate for long, I can see you don't want me in here and I damn sure don't want to be here. I am tired and I've had a bad day. All I want to do is make this bed, find my co-defendant, and use the phone."

Tracy said, "A big red lady, yeah, I know her. She works in the kitchen and lives in Unit 1, for the long timers. If you get ten years or more, they put you over there. You must not have a lot of time."

"Oh yeah, I got a lot of time."

She said, "What do you call a lot of time? You would not be over here if you had more than 10 years."

"Lady, I have forty to life sentence, is that enough time for you?"

All she could say was "Oh, Shit! You have to be telling a lie! I am so sorry, Cooper... I had no idea. Man, why did they give you all that? ... Look, finish making your bed and I am going to go and find. Ms. Mary and let her know you're here."

Tracy wasn't even gone five minutes and I could hear her saying "Hey, Coop!" So, I walked toward the door, looking for Tracy. "Ms. Mary is on her way over here; she is outside waiting on you!" Tracy yelled.

"Okay, thank you."

"Coop, look, we kinda got off on the wrong foot. Let's start over" Tracy said to me.

"Sure, no problem" I said to her and then went out the door and Mary stood there, smiling.

I hugged her and said, "Girl, I missed you."

"I've been waiting on you. What happened?" said Mary

"Well, it's a long story, I'll tell you about it."

"So, look, I already got it set up with your counselor and you will be moving over here with me."

"That is good."

She told me to go with her and I walked over to her unit. I asked her, "Where is the officer station?"

"Girl, the officer only comes over here when we have mail call and to count. The only other time we see an officer is when we call them."

"What do you mean, when you call them?"

She pointed to the phone on the wall. "You call them on that phone right there."

"So, there is never an officer in the unit unless it's mail call, count, or when you call them?

I SUPPORT HER

"That's right" Mary said. "Also, when we have a visit, they call us on the phone and whoever is the closest to the phone answers it and yells for whoever the phone is for. I know it's different from where we just left from, but Pam, (Mary always called me Pam instead of Coop) it's not bad, for real. It shouldn't take no more than a couple of days before they move you over here. The only thing I don't like is the snow! And girl, listen, when using the phone to call home, you can only make collect calls."

"What!"

"Yeah, that's the way it's set up here and they have HBO one and two. And girl, you don't have to go to bed if you don't want to. You can stay up all night long, as long as you get up and go to work the next day. Come on, I'll show you my room.

We went around to the left and up the hall. Her room was the second one. The door looked like the SHU door. It's heavy metal with a square glass window. She pulled it open and when I tell you that everything in there was red! Red bed spread, red curtains, a red rug, red toilet seat, and even red toilet paper!!! I mean, Mary went RED CRAZY! Let me explain this red obsession to you. On the street, she was called Lady Red. So, in prison, she feels that she is still, Lady Red. Now, I am standing here, thinking, I know she don't expect me to live in all this red shit! Well, guess what? Yes, she did.

Looking at me, Mary said "Well, what do you think? They let us do what we want with our room. Did you know that you can order silk sheets? I just ordered some red ones.

"Oh, really? Red? I would have never expected you to pick the color red!

She looked at me and said, "Oh, what a smart ass!"

"Yeah, that would be me. Look, Mary, let me get on out of here."

"Okay, well don't forget your bag." She had me some shower shoes, soap, lotion, a comb, a perm kit, a pair of sweats, sweatshirt, and some tennis shoes.

Man, she did good! "I said, "alright, Mary, thanks! Hey, what is upstairs?" She said there were more rooms and the Dr. Monroe..." Who is Dr. Monroe? I asked Mary.

"Oh, he counsels all the bulldoggers."

"Stop, playing!"

Mary said "For real, you will see what I mean when you move over here. Girl, it is crazy."

"So, Mary, you like working in the kitchen?"

"Yeah, and Pam, the food is so good. You can't beat the salad bar and, in the morning, I want you to come to breakfast. Man, they have any brand of cereal you could ever want. The kitchen foreman is so nice, he's saved. He got this copy of a book and he gives it to everybody. It's by some guy named Smith Wigglesworth. A lot of girls have read it already. Oh, and girl, talk about having church. They have good church. People be falling out and everything."

I SUPPORT HER

I said, "Please! Anyways, let me get back over there, I'll be seeing you! Later"

I started back to my unit and remembered I didn't have any cigarettes. I was getting ready to turn around and have Mary borrow me a pack of Newports from somebody. Then a girl came out of unit one and said, "Hey, your name is Pam, right?

"Yeah"

She said, "My name is Barbara, Ms. Mary told me to give these to you and these matches.

I smiled and said, "Thank you, I was just about to turn around and have Mary borrow me a couple of packs."

Barbara said "Ms. Mary said you would probably come back for some cigarettes and she was right."

"Thank you, again"

"Oh, you are welcome"

She started to walk off, but she turned around and said, "Hey, Pam, would you like to go to church with me?"

I told her, "No, maybe next time. Thank you anyway." I went and sat on one of the benches and smoked a cigarette. While I was smoking, I was thinking, "Why did she ask me that? I just got here. Man, look at this place. Where the hell am I and why am I here? I am a black snow bunny and its cold as hell here." I finished my cigarette and went inside.

I SUPPORT HER

When I walked in the door, a girl was coming out of the phone booth. I asked her, excuse me was somebody behind you? She turned and looked, "No, go ahead"

I went and called Linda and I didn't get an answer. So, I called my mama. When she answered, she said "Hi, Lil Lin!

I said "No, Mother, it's not Lil Lin, it's Pam."

"Oh, Lord!" she said. "Hi baby, how are you doing? Linda went to go see you, but you weren't there. I've been worried about you. Where are you baby?

"I am in Danbury, Mother, but don't have a choice."

"Are you okay, baby?"

"Yes, I am alright, don't start worrying. Have you heard anything from Shon?"

"Yeah, baby, he told me tell you that he's doing okay and don't worry. He, Lester, and Lenzy hang together and they are looking out for each other. He also said, there is a lot of people that he knows, and that he's going to be just fine."

"Oh, Mother, you don't know how happy I am to hear that. I have been so worried about him. He is only a kid. Hey, you said Linda came to see me?"

"Yeah, baby, she took her vacation and said she was going to see you, then she called and said that you had moved. I was so worried baby, because I didn't know where you were."

I SUPPORT HER

"Mother, I am so sorry for worrying you, but I am doing alright. Is Linda still in California?"

"No, baby, she came back yesterday."

"Did she have fun? I wish I had known she was going to come and see me. I would have called her and told her not to come. I really wish I could have seen her."

"Baby, she was very disappointed"

"I know, well, Mother, let me go, I don't want to run your phone bill up, and all calls from here are collect so you take care and don't worry; me and Shon are going to be fine, I promise. I love you, lady.

"I love you too, baby."

"Bye, Mother."

"Bye, baby"

I hung up and stood there looking at the phone for a while. I held my head down. Going over the conversation, then a girl came up from behind me and said, "Excuse me are you done with the phone?" I told, "Her yeah, I am through, go ahead." She said, "If you were going to make another call, I can wait." I said, "Oh no, I was just thinking about the conversation I just had with my mama. I am okay, for real, go ahead. I'll be alright."

She said, "My name is Tonya, what is your name?

I said, "Cooper. Pamela Cooper,"

I SUPPORT HER

Coming home from prison was like what you see in the movies. Sometimes the door doesn't just swing open to freedom. When I was released from prison, I had to spend over 6 months in a halfway house. Of course, I was excited to be from behind bars and closer to home, but I was confronted with new obstacles I had to overcome. Personal time was pretty much nonexistent, curfews were strict and the freedom I pictured was nothing like what I was experiencing. Luckily, my frustration turned to motivation.

It was a cultural shock. I didn't have anyone to walk me through what had taken place in society – 21 years have now passed. I felt so embarrassed. I felt that I was rushed into society instead of walking and taking my time. You are around people when you get out of prison that communicate on a totally different level, and often forget you have no clue of what they are even speaking. I needed someone to say, 'Pam, take your time. Do this and not that.' 'Let me show you.

As a red-blooded woman, I wanted – hell, needed – to feel love. Who am I kidding? I needed a hot body, a warm hug, and a plumber. One of the biggest mistakes I made was jumping into a relationship. I've been away from male companionship for 21 years and man was a total distraction. I wish I would have waited until I was more stable. I had to learn how to deal with my own anger. How to deal with the cloud over my head. I have to keep telling myself.... *"You are worthy."*

I wanted and needed my children, how I couldn't force on being a parent. I couldn't just come in and say, "I'm your mother. I want to be a part of your daily life. I want to be part of your extended family's lives. And I respect the idea that you may not want to call me dad. I understand because I haven't been here for you."

I SUPPORT HER

You make your kid understand. Be honest with your kids, man. Once you are honest with your kids, you can deal with whatever is coming. I eventually learned discipline and patience throughout the process.

CHAPTER 5

The Box on the Shelf

"Surviving Unspeakable Loss"

By: Danielle Ferreira

The emotional blow related to the loss of a child can trigger a wide range of psychological and physiological problems, including anxiety, depression, stress and marital issues. It increases the risk for suicide, guilt, and physical pain. All of these problems can persist long after the child's death and may potentially lead to diagnosable psychiatric conditions such as PTSD Post Traumatic Syndrome Disorder. It's been said that one of the most significant traumas imaginable is the death of a child or children, and some may say more stressful than the death of a parent or spouse. Because it is often unexpected; it is also in violation of the "usual" order of things, in which the child is expected to bury the parents.

I dedicated this chapter to all the arms left empty.

To the angels named and unnamed watching us every day. Finally, to you! You helped me to see a part of myself I was afraid to show. May you find the same peace you helped me to find?

To say I was completely surprised would be an understatement! I laid motionless for a moment before I began laughing so hard, I couldn't breathe. "Are you kidding me, you are joking, right? I just had a baby a year ago, and now you're telling me I'm not just expecting one but two babies? "Yep, fraternal twins," said the doctor. I jokingly asked the doctor for some smelling salts to use on my husband while I break the news. Henry, my then husband, was at home, making moving arrangements for our upcoming Military transfer to Virginia. We had enough on our plate, and now comes this. My mind became occupied with worry and doubt, as I thought about my next military assignment. I was reporting into a new engineering command, not to mention an entirely new branch of service arriving pregnant was the last thing I wanted to do. My current situation now changed my readiness status, and has now placed me on medically limited light-duty status. How is this going to look? I didn't want to be judged automatically. I didn't want to downgrade my blessing and complain; however, the last thing I wanted was to be viewed as weak, limited, and useless. I sat there for a moment, shocked and disappointed at the sheer timing of it all. It's hard enough having to deal with and overcome the normal, yet negative stereotypes concerning women in the military now add color to the mix, and don't forget into a male-dominated field of engineering. A white male-dominated field at that! I wasn't looking forward to walking in an automatic liability. I already understood the black tax I would have to pay; you know the typical get up earlier leave later work harder to get the same or less respect. And now this!

I drove home in silence, rehearsing how I was going to break the news to Henry. As I made it back, I walked into his typical jokes about "How did it go, punk?"

"Did the doctors tell you to lose weight?" I was always super stressed about my weight even though I was 15% body fat.

"Ha Ha! Nope."

"I don't have to lose no weight, nor workout any time soon." Henry looked perplexed. "Wait, what"? He saw that I had a lot of medical literature and a whole bag of goodies in my hands.

It was almost like he knew but didn't want to ask or hear the answer. Playing around and wreathing like we always did, I playfully placed one of the ultrasound pictures in its pocket. He reached in and said, "O what the F! Damnit Danielle!"

"No 'Damnit Danielle' Damnit Henry!"

"So, I can get the last laugh," I told him "go head look closer. There you go." I pushed his head down…a little closer. "What is that on the side are you okay, is it a growth?" "Nope! That's two babies." He grabbed the car keys pale face and drove to the store.

Once arriving at Portsmouth, Virginia, we reported in for my new arrival OB/GYN check-in appointment. Due to being pregnant with twins a therefore classified as high risk, they had to perform a completely new physical and ultrasound, even though I just had one. Thank God this was protocol for the reason that during the original ultrasound, it was noticed that our twins were fraternal, but now this ultrasound was showing the twins were not fraternal at all but identical twins. They began taking what felt like hundreds of measurements and pictures, to the point I was getting a little impatient. Upon further investigation, what was now identified as

Baby A was slightly smaller than Baby B. If that wasn't enough of a surprise, it appeared I had a condition known as Twin-to-Twin Transfusion Syndrome, or TTTS. They explained that TTTS is a rare, yet serious condition that can occur in pregnancies when identical twins share a placenta. The abnormal blood vessels connections form in the placenta and allow blood to flow unevenly between the babies. One twin, usually the larger twin – called the donor – becomes dehydrated. The other named recipient – develops high blood pressure and produces too much urine and overfills the amniotic sac. Unfortunately, without treatment, approximately 70–80% of twins with TTTS will die. Survivors may have injuries to their brains, hearts, and kidneys. Fetal deaths are typical between 17 to 26 weeks gestation in monochromic twins complicated by TTTS.

I considered myself a keen woman; however, I found myself having a hard time making sense of anything that I had just heard.

What should have been a quick and easy 45 minutes, welcome to Portsmouth Naval Hospital OB/GYN appointment and tour, soon turned into a 3-hour appointment filled with devastating news followed up by strict do's and don'ts. Dr. Eggleston placed his hand on my shoulder and said, "By the way, you are now on COMPLETE – and I mean complete – bed rest." My husband and I both mindlessly staring at him with open mouths, he broke it down in military terms. "I mean complete bed-rest, to only SS&S – shit, shave and shower! You are also to report here for all check-ups (mandatory), no matter what it is, the medical clinic on base is not equipped to handle your situation."

We remain sitting there, frozen as everything but the kitchen sink was thrown at us. When I thought it couldn't get any worse, they gave us the option to do the following.

First choice reduction, meaning (pick a twin to tie off the umbilical cord to allow the baby to slowly die within your womb) Second choice, terminate both and finally the last choice, do nothing, receive proper treatment and continue with the pregnancy. I got angry. With all things considered, how could I...could we...choose that? How do you pick one? What!? By default, do you select the smaller twins because, at that time, he or her chances appears hopeless? Terminating was not an option, so we decided to continue with the pregnancy and fight. I begin to cry, the type of cry when you are completely wiped out. The remainder of my day consisted of blood draws, urine screens, and a nutrition consultation. Most women with TTTS experience malnourished anemia and low blood protein during their mid-pregnancy. The doctors discussed it with me all in great detail.

Due to the severe morning sickness, my calorie intake would become closely monitored. Dehydration was also a significant risk, so I had to double my water intake even if I couldn't keep it down. They gave me a stack of coupons and samples of Boost, Carnation Instant Breakfast, and Ensure Plus. It was highly recommended I drink at least three cans per day. I was placed on a high protein diet. I was given instructions on how to sit, rest, and sleep in bed horizontally to reduce pressure on the cervix. I was shown how to lie on my side correctly while on the couch, bed, recliner, or floor when playing with my kids. Also, resting horizontally improves blood flow to the uterus, which was super important. I was now at information overload. Words ran from my ears. I wished I had four new arms to carry all the paperwork, books, and other stuff we received. I remember looking at Henry, and all I could say is "Damn! Welcome to Virginia."

I felt like a referee during this pregnancy as the babies battled it out inside. One week it was Baby A, taking all the nutrition. The next week Baby B. As they would fight, the weaker twin would feed on the host. That host was me. I became very ill; I retain water in my legs and feet to the point I couldn't put on my shoes. I couldn't hold nothing down, and I mean nothing, so to ensure proper nutrition I had an IV going into my stomach due to Hyperemesis gravidarum, I threw up as many as 10 or 20 times a day and was unable to keep anything down. I became severely dehydrated, weak, and exhausted. I had an IV bag on the timer on my person at all times. If that wasn't bad enough, I began losing my hair. I became too depressed every time I looked in the mirror. I appeared more and more drained.

I struggled to keep my appearance from dictating my worth as a person, as a woman – but it was hard. It was often told to me: it's just hair. Friends and family would say, "Your hair grows back fast, Danielle, it will be alright." There were true, but mostly unhelpful and unsupportive tidbits. But my hair just kept coming out – in my comb, the shower, stuck between my bra strap my back, my pillow and pretty much every surface in our home. The worst was hair falling in my mouth as I try to eat and drink. On top of the list of side effects, my blood pressure was becoming unstable. They were killing me! I was their mother, and I was going to fight, and fight hard, to keep them healthy. During one of my appointments, it was apparent that the dehydration started. My stomach became large and bruised. The recipient twin, whose system was becoming overwhelmed by too much fluid, began producing more urine than usual. This eventually led to an enlarged bladder and excess amniotic fluid. The excess fluid can strain the recipient twin's heart, sometimes leading to heart failure. It was recommended I begin the treatment of amnioreduction under an ultrasound-guided needle placement ASAP, so I did. The procedure, amnioreduction, drained the excess amniotic fluid from the recipient twin's sac, with hopes of improving blood flow.

The doctor explained that a long needle that can vary in gauges (typically 18 or 20 gauge), varying amounts of fluid that needs to be removed. Under sterile conditions, the needle was placed into my stomach. The treatment was risky mainly due to contractions risk premature labor, spontaneous rupture of the membrane, or chorioamnionitis (infection of the fetal member). Still, it was a necessary treatment to increase survival, to ease the pressure I was feeling in my abdomen and to reduce the stress on the twins. I had consented to having the amniotic fluid removed and measured every other day or, as needed, this placed me under a lot of stress. During the procedure, I'd spent so much time worrying about labor, fearing blood infection from needles, but while in the moment, when they warned the needle would "feel cold and scratchy, then burn and sting, so brace yourself," I didn't care. "Just tell me when it's over."

After the treatment, I would rub my belly, searching for any signs of life after. As things progressed, my physical condition was becoming worst, and so was the twin's health. My doctor informed us about a surgery that could improve their situation and give the twins an improved 80- 90% survival rate. When babies are more severely affected by TTTS, the team may recommend elective surgery. The surgery, known as Selective Fetoscopic Laser Photocoagulation (Laser Surgery) it had a very high success rate. This procedure would've involved making a small incision in my abdomen and inserting a trocar, or small metal tube, into the uterus. The surgeon would then pass a fetoscope (a kind of medical telescope) through the metal tube to see all of the blood vessel connections on the surface of the placenta shared by the twins. After all of the abnormal blood vessel connections are identified, the laser is applied to seal shut these vessels and disconnect them permanently.

"WOW, that sounds great, right?"

For the first time in a long time, we felt hopeful we felt alive. We have a real plan! He then informs us that the surgery was viewed by the Military as experimental. All this means is we have to get permission by Military Medical standards board approval. The burden was then placed on my doctor to prove, more like beg and convince the medical board members that this selective Fetoscopic Laser Photocoagulation (Laser Surgery) was necessary for the survival of my twins. Dr. Eggleston was very prepared. He took extensive evidence that all of the other procedures performed within my treatment plan had failed and or have shown little to no improvement or results in the twin condition. Again, WE had a plan!

Henry and I were both thrilled to see the excitement on our doctor face as he wished us luck. Dr. Eggleston had an excellent bedside manner, so I felt comfortable and trusted that he was totally on our side. Knowing he worked diligently to submit proven medical research, doctor's letters, and medical records in support of my request, took a mighty load off my mind and heart. But most importantly, I was relieved at the very thought of I will no longer have to deal with the pain, risk and discomfort of that amnioreduction procedure. The needle posed more and more of a risk entering into my body, even though this procedure is performed under sterile conditions, the risk of infection and premature labor is great.

We sat on pins and needles anticipating the verdict from the medical board. Every time the phone rang, I jumped. A week has now passed, when the phone rang, we were finally told to come in. We have taken this route many times, but this time it took forever. I didn't say a word holding back tears, praying. We finally arrived and was quickly ushered to the office. I sat there shaking, holding his hands so tight, his fingers tips were white. I think I went deaf after I heard our request was denied twice. The first denial was quick; our application was automatically resubmitted. It was their opinion the laser treatment wasn't beneficial and to continue with current treatment, Amnioreduction! Even though my pain was increasing and premature labor was inevitable.

My mouth hung open as I walked, crying; I couldn't breathe! I was disgusted and tried hard not to focus on the blatant disregard for my health. How could they say no to a request like this? Why would they say no? The board decided that the twins were not going to be dying at that very moment and give the current treatment plan a little more time to turn things around. They were wrong, the twins and I were dying a little each day. Negative emotions overtook me. It's just female problems! I say, its only female issues! Right? I became angry, as I thought about countless women getting denied medical treatments, or any treatment for that matter. It was a fact that women have a higher denial rate than ANY issue surrounding our male counterparts. It was known and proven that female issues get pushed aside until we were fighting for our lives with baseball-sized cysts, bleeding internally with chronic or debilitating pain. If women cry or express concern, it was often said or implied that women are overreacting and are soon to be brushed off, misdiagnosed, or provided the wrong treatment. But the worse, the famous words "Take two of these, and report back to FULL duty, ASAP!" "Hell, women don't want special care; we just want the same level of quality care that the men have." I looked at my husband and said, "Let a penis go limp! George Washington himself would rise from the dead only to sign an executive order in support of the penis. It would be lifted painted and crowned as GOD! If there were a known experimental procedure that would prevent sexual disruptions in men, I bet the board would have a UNANIMOUS vote." Henry looked at me, said nothing. His eyes said it all as he nodded his head in agreement. But the reality remained that this was not for a man nor a penis, it was for my babies, and the answer received will be still no, so I became bitter!

My condition grew worse with complications of anemia, hypertension preeclampsia, intrahepatic cholestasis (ICP), and polyhydramnios. I started noticing swelling in my hands and face, mild at first but as we progressed it became more and more pronounced. I started vomiting and was experiencing sharp pains in my upper right quadrant

In my case, I was dealing with extreme fetal tissue swelling, called hydrops. I became at risk for maternal "mirror" syndrome, a condition that mimics that of the sick fetus. Because of a high-flow, high-volume cardiovascular state, I develop symptoms that are similar to preeclampsia — that included vomiting, hypertension, generalized body swelling (more so than usual), excessive protein in the urine (proteinuria), and dangerous build-up of fluid in my lungs (pulmonary edema). Soon after, more and more Emergency Department visits, severe shortness of breath, elevated blood pressure, and bilateral lower limb edema. AKA Severe swelling everywhere.

Henry, missed more and more work became unable to stand duty. Lucky for him he was a part of an excellent command. His Commanding Officer sat up a special duty section to help watch our children assist around the home with chores so he could pay full attention to me.

A command representative called every day, letting us know they were thinking of and praying for us! On the flip side, my command was the exact opposite. They only called to demand me to come to work against doctor's orders just to look at me. "We need to see you physically." Now, keep in mind, I was on strict bed rest. Getting out of bed would place me in great danger. When I would respectfully remind them of my medical restrictions and mandatory instruction, I was undermined, they would push back with, "That's a Navy doctor's instructions, and not a Coast Guard one." I was shocked and laughed at the pure stupidity at this point. The Coast Guard is the smallest branch of services, and have no official Military Hospital; Coast Guardsman must receive treatment from the other military medical facilities sponsored by the other branches. So, they forced me to report by threatening my career and Henry's career. They forced me first to stop in to see them, the command, and then into a Coast Guard unequipped clinic. This became an unbearable stressor for me that increased blood pressure was making me both weak and sick. As we battled my command, we were still fighting for our lives, preparing for an emergency medical board appeal. Over time, this consistent abuse of power had gotten to the point where an official complaint was needed. We also enlisted the support from his command and the NAVY. We were blessed that Portsmouth Naval Command Master Chief (USCG) Bernard Cofield, stepped in and took care of our concerns, easing our burden and getting us out of unnecessary direct danger. A true GOD send.

It was May 4th, 2002. I woke up with the arm, neck and lower back pain. The kids started a bath so I can relax. Shortly after, I felt dizzy and sick. My eyes rolled to the back of my head. I felt my husband pull me out of the tub. As he began scrambling to get me to dress, the kids called the doctor ordering us to report to the ER; I was admitted and taken straight through to intensive care. Once I arrived, a tube was placed in my nose to my stomach, urine catheter, blood tested, and finally resting at a 45 degrees angle to help prevent premature labor. I was pinned to the bed with machines. If something was to happen, I wasn't afraid of feeling pain. I was scared they were going to be pulled from my body, lifeless. I wouldn't hear them cry. Until, this!

"Henry, your wife is going into premature labor." I can't believe this is happening now. The doctor yelled, "She's going into labor." Hearing these words sound as if it was a dramatic line from a movie. There was no way I am having these babies at 27 weeks! It's too early and yet, it was happening, and now. Then five doctors and three nurses arrived and confirmed and reconfirmed it. "There's nothing else you can do to stop this?" "No, there's nothing else." The boys were coming whether I liked it or not.

In pure panic, he yelled, "I'm so sorry, Mama. Danielle! Danielle! We have to do this now; I'm sorry I'm so sorry. Please understand!" As the nurse changed my IV, I was covered in sweat, exhausted, and confused by the sheer panic that was happening around me. I spun around, searching for my husband's face, only to see in his eyes a level of pure fear I never saw before. I heard the rips from my hospital gown that was being removed. I was thrown, pulled, repositioned; thrown, pulled and repositioned again as doctors begin to surround, and now hover over me. I felt as if I was in a tunnel. Stainless trays fill with tools IV bags ripped opened and hung, I couldn't breathe as tears rolled down my face. Due to my high-risk pregnancy and the frequent hospital visits, we became like family and on a first name basis to a few doctors and nurses. So, I wasn't surprised in the amount of people running to touch my face forehead hand and arms, the last bit of comfort before the sharp poke. I started to panic and then listened intently to everything that was being said, as if I understood what they were talking about; but I was too scared to let myself sleep. Suddenly I woke up in what I thought was a war zone, unfamiliar voices, and screams. I felt so much pain, "She's up." The nurse administers additional meds taking me under. I suddenly felt nothing. I was surrounded by warmth and white. I heard a small ringing in my ears then nothing. Just like that, my pain had gone. All the discomfort was now gone. All the fear, sadness, and worry were gone. I just felt so incredibly light, happy. A complete moment of unconditional love. Without warning, I saw a figure standing to my left, and the vision became clear

"Grand-dad," I yelled.

He smiled and gave me a quick once over; we talked about everything. Sometimes communication without words or movement. Note my granddad has been dead for many years now. His presence felt like hours. My Granddad placed his hand on my shoulder "You must go now."

"Why?" I asked. "I have so much to tell you."

"You can't stay here; you have plenty to do."

I SUPPORT HER

"Do it!"

I felt deep pain first, starting in my chest then a burning sensation covered my body. I began seeing a short burst of images then nothing. It wasn't until later I found out I died not once, but twice, on the table. Antonio Ferreira was born at a mere 1.7kgs, the gestational size of a 19-week-old. Mercifully he was breathing well, but because of his low birth weight, was taken straight to the special care unit. Alexandro Ferreira was born at 1 pound; he was breathing as well; however, was slowly dying. I awoke to blurry images and quite a conversation. I tried to speak, looking around the room for my babies. When my voice was finally able to be heard, I softly asked for my babies. No one answered. I asked again and again when I heard someone yell.

"Push the button!"

I felt sleepy. I woke again now screaming for my babies. My eyes struggled a little to focus, as Henry handed me a beautiful basket with one of my baby boys inside. Beautiful black hair, tiny hat, and soft gown. Soft blankets. I was so happy I saw the movement of his little hand. I yelled out, "Thank you, GOD! He made it!" Everyone in the room was silent. Henry softly said, "Baby. Honey, look at me. He's gone, my love." I pulled my shoulder away from him. "What the hell do you mean he's GONE? He's moving. He's F&$ moving!" I heard someone say, "It's the meds, we should put her back under." I fell asleep. I woke up to a different blanket, with a beautiful little boy. I thought I was in the twilight zone; I felt I was dreaming. This cannot be true. I'm dreaming. I'm going crazy. NO; I am insane. They are alive. It took three days to fully understand that the twins were indeed dead. At that very moment, I, understandably, emotionally collapsed. I want GOD to take me. I didn't deserve to live. My grief crowded my heart, ate up all my emotional energy, and chronically imposed upon my peace. I was confused, lost the ability to concentrate, feeling that I was going crazy.

Leaving the hospital

We lost them! It was the hardest thing we've been through. We had to explain to our children what happened. We thought we had more time to prepare, but we didn't. I felt robbed of 3 months of pregnancy and growth, and deprived of our precious twin boys. I felt cheated by the organization I faithfully served. You cannot imagine the feeling of walking out of the hospital after giving birth and not taking your babies home in their car seats with you. All I could carry out with me was flowers and two memory boxes. It took stone-cold concentration to put one foot in front of the other while people were staring at me; required all of my energy to not collapse on the floor hysterically kicking, screaming and crying. At the same time, warm tears rolled down my face, and I managed to get to the car and once in reminded myself to breathe. Just breathe.

The Mothers

Henry's mother, Dora, came up to assist with our children, household tasks, and of course me. She was a much needed help, and the kids enjoyed having their grandmother around. She cooked and cleaned and kept the boys out of Henry way so he could rest his body and mind. He started to look very pale due to no sleep and stress. I still wasn't feeling well dealing with a lot of pain, so my doctor ordered little to no movement, so I was bedridden again. Smells of Spanish food filled the air; my mouth would water, yet I was not hungry. I felt I didn't deserve to eat. My body failed me, so why should I feed it? I was so disappointed in my failure to carry them to the full term. So, my body didn't deserve anything! She would come up with rice and beans and pleaded with me to eat when I refused; she'd fuss with Henry until he couldn't take it no more and begged me to eat. "Please take one bite. You know she's not going to stop worrying," he would say. Several times a day, Henry had to give me my meds and perform wound care, looking for any signs of infection and repacking them from the infected C-section cut. I was still so weak, mentally tired, and didn't understand – nor did I want to understand – how I was feeling inside. I wanted to die, as I filled my pillow with tears while running down the list of... if I would have drunk enough milk; did I get enough rest; did I take enough vitamins? As the days rolled on, I found myself becoming very angry that she was here. She became a real reminder of what I didn't have. Even though I was so very grateful and genuinely appreciated everything, she did for me. Still, I felt envious. I was jealous that Henry had a mother that loved him liked no other. I wanted that for myself wishing deep inside, she belonged to me, that she was my mom. I cried at night; I was so embarrassed in front of his family that my side was nowhere near that close, considerate or caring.

As a woman and a mother, I am always surrounded by reminders that my mom should be my best friend. I'm often bewildered by the natural bond that mothers and daughters have and found myself wondering what was wrong with me. I can say I had an unhappy/ happy upbringing, which depended sorely on who I was around. I wasn't particularly always pleased as a child of feeling very neglected. I was clothed, fed, and had ballet lessons, yet my mother and I never had the closeness I saw in my friends' relationships. Especially my white friend's. They would share with their mom's things about their lives, their dreams. When I tried to ask my mother about her teenage years and upbringing, she told me to mind my own business. So, I did. I grew up minding my own business, and she minded hers. So, my mother was, and is the last person I go to in a crisis. She is undoubtedly the last person to whom I would tell a secret or a problem. When I say that I don't have a close relationship with her, it was immediately followed up with questions, long faces, concern, and pity.

The Viewing the Funeral & Henry

At the viewing is when everything around me just disappeared as I held on to their cold, lifeless bodies. At times, I still saw them move. I found myself whispering, did anyone notice that? I would hear cries and feel movement within my stomach. I was being told this was all in my head. There's only so many times you can be told that before you start to think you're going crazy. I was frail, almost back down to pre-pregnancy weight due to not eating. I cried, rolled, and sat still; cried, turned and sat still again. I was praying that I get thought the funeral. I felt like Henry had to hide how heartbroken he was to be the strong one looking after the family's emotional needs. He wouldn't tell me when he felt upset because he didn't want to upset me. I thought we were dealing with this together, right? It has now become difficult to speak. Why couldn't we share in each other's grief? I guess we shared it intimately but dealt with it differently. No one prepares you for the many different stages of grief, anger and the blame game. I was mad with an emotional train wreck, because I didn't get the closure I needed – the closure I deserved. I felt tricked, lied to! Cheated by God. When I tried to express my feeling to him, it was matched with his passion. It started to feel like a tug-of-war and battle of who felt more hurt or who suffered more? When he would get angry, he would say, "You didn't have to watch you die, RIGHT?!" "You didn't have to give comfort care to not only one, but two babies; I did!"

"You were OUT COLD! I had to deal with that! Me!" I would respond with the same amount of energy, yelling things like, "At least you saw them alive! They were dead. Dead; gone when I got them. DEEEEEEEEEEEAD!"

Major life stressors naturally take a toll on marriages. I began communicating poorly, not understanding the many different ways to deal with grief. Within my selflessness, I thought he wasn't as upset about our twin deaths as I was. He thought that, I was too emotional and will eventually begin taking time away from our children. It became difficult for me to understand he may not want to hear about my feelings so often, and accept that he may, at times, think I'll never truly get over my grief. There were times we both felt left out of all the support the other was receiving. There were times people would ask me how I was doing but often forgot to ask how he was doing. It slowly became common to place myself and my feelings above his. As a woman, there's a special bond with the baby during pregnancy. My twins were real to me; I felt every movement, every discomfort. In my heart, there will always be this unbreakable attachment. I told myself how he couldn't understand, all in an attempt to justify how I felt. He didn't carry the babies in his body, so the twins had to be less real to him, right? I tried convincing myself.

I found myself drowning, unable to celebrate as I have in the past. I was becoming more and more afraid to just live. Mother's Day's was difficult, I honestly didn't think it would be a struggle, but I wailed. I didn't feel like a mother, even though I had other children. My arms are still empty, and I have longed for them. I was always blaming myself even years later. I had to learn when faced with an overwhelming turn of events; it was okay to say, "I just can't think about all of this right now. I need time to work through what's happened and adapt to new circumstances." But then denial hit. I began pushing it out of my mind and creating a world of less feeling. Denial should only be a temporary measure — it won't change the reality of the situation. I was trying hard to protect myself. I wanted to protect myself by refusing to accept the truth about something that happened in my life. I did this over and over again. However, my short-term denial proved to be a good thing, giving me time to adjust, but my denial was unhealthy and how to move past it.

Refusing to acknowledge that something was wrong, the way I was coping with things was wrong. The emotional conflict of stress, painful thoughts, the threatening information I played over and over in my head. My anxiety grew, and as it grew, I found ways to build high walls around these issues, hide these issues. Feeling vulnerable was not an option. I was told to move past it, pray about it go to church more. All of which made the situation WORSE; this advice usually came from people that had no real clue of how you felt.

The nightmare became I whole new challenge, they would greet me live and in living color, smells, and sounds. The one that played the most is me lying on my back staring at the ceiling, I can hear the sounds of the hospital machine beeping, people talking in corridors and I see imagines of busyness from the operating and treatment rooms. Then the voices. My heart would begin beating, matched by rapid breathing. I will look over at Henry's sad and sympathetic face. He will look helpless as he slowly mouthed the words their dead. Then, without waiting his face would change, and I would hear him say, "You're a bad mother, you couldn't even carry them. Can you do anything right?" As I awake screaming and crying. I felt that I was not normal. I was afraid and terrified. I was stuck. Walking around in my feelings. When people interacted with me, I would seem present for them; but for me, I was still be living in the past. A living history that torments me over and over again.

Moving on

During my post-natal appointments. I became one of THOSE patients. You know the ones; the anxiety would be through the roof when I see a nurse or doctor, any type of medical equipment. My hands would be sweaty, my mind would be racing a million miles per hour, and my heart would feel like it is about to explode out of my chest. I would want to throw up. I would clench onto my handbag ever so tight. Holding on for dear life once I stepped into the exam room. The distinct smell of the waiting room has me on high alert. I smelled it as soon as I walked in, as soon as I opened the door. Disinfectant. You won't notice it – you are accustomed to the sterile smell. For most, the scent probably reassures that you're safe. Safe from disease and bacteria, but for me it is the first sign of danger my body experiences when I come for a visit. My body wants to run. The sounds of footsteps get louder and louder. I experienced over alertness felt on the edge panicking, when reminded of them I could no longer sleep.

I became easily upset. I thought I was coping well. Shortly after the loss, I began experiencing unpleasant physical symptoms, comparable to those of a heart attack: chest pain, tightness, and dizzy spells so severe that I thought I would pass out. My heart was always racing, and I felt permanently dizzy. I couldn't leave the house without help and became afraid of going to sleep, as I was convinced that they were in the other room. I was convinced I heard their cries. I saw myself die over and over again. I wanted to die. I felt as if I had a leg on each side of a dark invisible timeline, where the past pulled me in one direction and the present another. I rehearsed all the normal should-of, could-of. I saw flashes of dark images and heard sounds that came out of nowhere; my heart raced, and my breathing was loud, I no longer understood my behavior, nor my family. Who was I? My belief changed and I became erratic, depressed.

After a year, I would alternate between wanting to shut myself off from the world, from family and friends and being around people. Sometimes, I didn't want to see or talk to anyone or be around them. Other times, I would stay out late in store parking lots, just sitting in my car. I was also still deeply depressed, and experiencing massive amounts of anxiety. I refused to go anywhere alone or go near any babies especially twins they freaked me out. But what was sadder, no one could tell. I can say due to my childhood I learned all too well how to bottle up my feelings and place my energy elsewhere, HENCE why I was a super performer at work. Work became my pain reliever; I was already a top performer but now I was SUPER SAILOR. Work became my GOD; and I associated family with anxiety and fear; fear of losing them. If they were to get sick, OMG, the world came to an end, my mind would think the worst.

Suicidal Thoughts and PTSD.

I developed PTSD and post-natal anxiety and referred myself to a psychologist. The lack of information and support for women who have had a similar experience astounds me. I could never fix my lips to admit that I was feeling hopeless and filled with self-criticism. It was becoming harder to enjoy and experience pleasurable emotions from life events such as eating, exercise, or social interaction. The guilt was taking over, and because I had no true outlet, I started bottling things up more and more while wearing a happy go lucky mask. I know now I began killing myself long before then, by the apparent stuff. Not feeding my body the healthy foods I needed, not feeding my mind and refusing to feed my spirit. Whenever I attempted to speak to someone about how I was feeling, they could never listen without judgment or the miss "ME TOO," and the "I got over it, why can't you" stuff. Taking the advice of family and friends, I attempted to go back to church for healing. So many times, I walked away feeling worst and suicidal! I can recall sharing with a member how I was feeling and was told "Child, that's the devil, those feelings are "NOT of GOD"... you got to get your life right," but had no real advice on how to get there. My great grandfather built his church from the ground up. So, I was not new to the faith and understood how to pray; however, these holier-than-thou church fools almost lead me to jump headfirst off a building. The church and its people were no longer choices for healing. So, I began seeking other forms for healing, who needs their guidance when you have a real prayer life! So, I did my own thang! I explore mindfulness and forced my mind on my awareness of the present moment.

Acknowledging and accepting my feelings, sensations, and thoughts began to improve my life. I included meditation and yoga. I was an Oprah freak and began following the many people who helped transform her life, like Mr. Deepak Chopra, Ms. Iyanla Vanzant. Mr. Wayne Dyer and Bishop T.D. Jakes, to name a few. I read books like *The Secret* and began the rebuilding of me!

If you want to know how I went about changing my story and what that looked like? Well, first, I had to make the most out of every day I made every day my day. I stopped complaining, never knowing what the next moment may bring, I had to learn to stop worrying about things I couldn't control. I reminded myself that living in a state of lack gives and creates more lack. I remember my grandmother's teaching and began tapping into my surroundings, genuinely understanding that GOD is everywhere, and in everything, no one has to teach you that all you have to do is listen! God provides everything you need, were born with it. I stop counting myself out. I muted the negative self-talk, blocked the self-doubt and self-defeating behavior. I appreciated everything about myself. WALKING, TALKING, BREATHING, LIVING, LOVING, and GROWING better every day. I had a whole new spiritual code and practice. This is how I change my story; this is how you can change yours. No one can change it but you. God has placed in us everything we need, life and godliness. Now understand, connecting the body mind and spirit was not easy.

We are so programmed to just pray about it and walk away without doing any work. So, I put in the work and more work and more work. I work on my energy, learning how to heal my mind, and each day I got a little better. I must say the crucial things to remember is you must first sit down, shut up listen get to know your spiritual channel. Keep a daily Journal…do not stay where you don't want to be because you convince yourself; you have no other place to go; I learn this from Iyanla Vanzant. If I didn't want to be sad unhappy depressed suicidal, I had to do the work. I had to be honest about my feelings and admit to my pain then ask for help! Again, be very honest about my feelings.

Today I want to help others, I want my story to educate people I want to tell you if you are reading this, it DOES get better and we are here for you. You can recover and heal from whatever holding you hostage. Even if its suicidal feelings and PTSD

A long journey it is, and will be. I want you to know how much I have achieved in such a small space of time. I want you to know with PTSD, there isn't a quick fix, and there is always a new hill to climb. With each leap, there are still some backward steps too. But the one thing I want you to know is that I am getting there! Remember this; you have to learn to recognize the many ways your pain, hurt and disappointment manifest themselves and acknowledge them, then FIX IT!

Resources

If you or your partner need support for a challenging birth experience, you can access ourPeer2Peer Support Service via greatpathwaycs.com
For more information about TTTS www.ttts.org

CHAPTER 6

Her Bleeding Heart Made Whole Again

"If God Saved Me, He Can Save You"

By: Albertina Dancy

Since the age of fifteen, after My father's death, I became bitter and wanted the same attention my father gave me. I was a daddy's girl. My father was the best a girl could ever have. The relationship we had no one could ever treat me like the queen I deserved to be like but him. Years went by as I searched for that kind of love; the kind I was familiar with. So here goes the downhill of my life. In my mind a thousand thoughts ran through. I was so concerned about failing again and people knowing my love life failed. I thought about how embarrassing it was to be married and on the verge of divorce in less than 10 months. I didn't give myself enough chance to heal before I was in another relationship that went sour. I was scared to heal and be alone. I thought maybe life is better without me around. I began to draw my bedroom curtains, refusing to eat for three days, lying in my bed. I felt sorry for myself. I stopped bathing, abandoning communications with my close friends because I was in a dark place feeling sorry for myself.

My current scars are a reflection of every premature decision I made without giving thought to the brutal consequences. It was July 7, 2013. It seemed like my days became shorter and my nights became longer...Before I knew it; I was watching the sunrise again... Listening to the rhythmic beat of my heart. "Lord, who am I? Is this the heart you created?" My heart couldn't take this kind of heartbreak anymore. I experience so many heartbreaks from dating to marriage. After two failed marriages, I begin to question myself, "Why me, Lord?" I cried out loud. I began to hyperventilate sobbing over another man that said he would never hurt me. He said he loved me and I never understood why the man before me mistreated me. I couldn't get my thoughts together. All I could think about was all the times I spent being a good wife in my marriage and phenomenal girlfriend to this man that I told all my pain of separation to. Only to find out he only wanted me for good time and security. "What makes me different than her?" "Why couldn't he be faithful to me?" I thought I was the best thing that ever happened to him. He told me I was beautiful. Overwhelmed with all those thoughts through my head and flashbacks of seeing her in my house, unexpectedly rubbing her stomach saying, "Your man is my baby's father." I lost every feeling I had. Stars and dark spots overtook my version as I began to storm out of my own apartment and drive off, empty inside. Numbing feeling is what I felt. I just wanted to drink my life away forgetting my faith in God. I thought to myself, "He let me go through this without saving me from hurt! God you knew I didn't want to be in pain again.

God you knew I wanted a man to love me for me, and give just as much respect and pampering as I would him." I promised myself I wouldn't allow pain to kill me. After returning back to my apartment that evening, the devil began to speak to me again. "End it all!" I rushed and found bottles of Oxycontin, Flexeril and Hydrocodone in my kitchen cabinet left over from previous surgeries. I was feeling so overwhelmed and depressed, I couldn't take it anymore. I started shaking nervously as I held all the pills in my hand taking them all down with water. As I laid down on my bed I immediately started to worry. It was too late, I overdosed.

I felt trapped in my own feelings. The thought of my mother knowing about this bothered me. How she would feel hearing about my death made me guilty about what I did. I immediately started praying, asking God to forgive and help me. My heart began to race, my vision became blurry, my body became numb as I struggled to call my only associate friend to come get me. " I overdosed on my pain pills please come get me". I'll never forget hearing my friend scream over the phone she was on the way to unlock the door. I remember walking from the bedroom to the front door to unlock wobbly and feeling very exhausted. I was so weak I fell over onto my sofa until they arrived. I remember my friend and her husband helping me to their car.

When I arrived at the emergency room I faded into a dark black tunnel. I couldn't remember anything else. Before I knew it, I was awake, surrounded by nurses and doctors at my bedside. My ears were closed to just a tunnel sound I could hear. My vision was blurry, but enough I could see the bright ceiling light and the pulling and grabbing on me as they started working on me quickly. Immediately I began to shake uncontrollably, I didn't know what I was going through. My body was doing its own thing and I could only hear the muffled voices saying "Relax!!!"I heard the beeping of the heart monitor going off. I slowly went into a deep sleep at that moment.

The next day I was placed in an observation triage room, I was woken by an older white gentleman sitting by my bedside. "What happened? Are you still feeling suicidal?" I was lost for words, I felt much better sitting up in my hospital bed. "I am fine and ready to go home". The gentleman explained that I was being assessed for the Crisis Unit. This man made me realize I was worth more than what could have cost me my life in Hell. "Young lady, you are too beautiful, intelligent to allow a heartbreak to ruin what future God has for you. Pick yourself up, I'll give you my number, seek some counseling to heal from your hurt. Never ever allow a man to control your mental stability." I cried so hard, because I realized how stupid I was. Because I work in the field of mental health as a clinician, it was so embarrassing to be sitting in front of my own fellow colleague. Although he didn't know me personally, he knew God and He ministered and prayed for me. I was discharged that afternoon from the hospital under his recommendation. "Young Lady, your heart is hurting but God is waiting to mMake you whole again." The gentleman departed my room.

Sitting up in my hospital bed, I began to reflect on all I allowed myself to go through. "That man made total sense to me!" It seemed like right away, I was able to reflect on my hurt without feeling emotional for the first time. I began to analyze the relationship. When I met this guy, I thought it was him, his sweet words made me believe in him...he loved me and finally I fell in love with him. I did everything to please him. I wanted to prove my love for him instead of him proving his love for me. I was too convinced that I no longer had to suffer from low self-esteem due to my previous relationship that I never had a chance to heal from. I sacrificed my life for him, allowing him in my personal space knowing deepest secrets. I gave up friendships and made him my sanctuary. I had forsaken God, and was doing what was best to please me. Now, he was aware of all the previous heart breaks and why I prefer to stay to myself.

How did I recover? I began to work on what I love to do best. Singing is therapy for me. It's like an escape from the present situation. Music releases all stress and began to be my coping strategy to better me. I began to seek counseling to work on my divorce and relationship hurts I never healed from. I started spending quality time talking to God and praying for guidance on what to do next in my healing process. As time went on, my relationship became consistent with him. For the very first time I experienced the sweet voice of GOD say:

"My child, cry no more after today, your season of heartbreak is over. You tried to end it all but I refused to let your ending be in your control. You tried to allow yourself to be the victim way too long in every relationship and marriage with men I never sent for you. I will heal you today, you will learn the strength of your struggles. You will have an eye to see what I want you to see. You will spend more time with me. Your relationship with me will become more intimate. Watch how I transform your heavy heart and hopeliness to peace, joy and love. I have work for you. I made you for ministry. I made you pray and hear my voice in a way of guidance. When I'm done reshaping and molding you, I will send the man I chose for you. If you become distracted by the temptations, I will always be here for you to start all over again. Understand and appreciate who I made you. Fall in Love with the person I made you. Slow down, make your experiences testimonies for others and watch how I create a glow on you that you won't even understand. In the midst of chaos, I will hide you in my shadows." I realize at that moment I couldn't blame the men I allowed to break my heart. I was responsible for not being wise in my decisions when signs of heartbreak were visible and I ignored them. I realize that GOD was always there. I chose to shut him off.

Every day l stand in front of a mirror and look at the beautiful woman that I never saw. In the beginning of my recovery process I didn't like all the imperfections but I made myself work on goals to reshape the woman I'm healing from today. I realized that I am in control of myself and although I was in recovery, I still failed two more times in relationships and a marriage once again but this time it didn't break me. GOD was right! he is always there. I realized after giving birth to two wonderful boys that they were my blessings and my relationship experiences were all a part of plan GOD. So "Okay GOD, I slipped again, I'm ready now to become the woman you created for me to be. I'm convinced GOD. your promises are true. You promise to give me peace and you have even through my current hurts. GOD you have caused every wanted tear to be joy and every victimized situation forgiving and a place of peace. So today, I tell my story of all of the times I have assassinated my own heart with what I wanted.

I am not perfect but I have a wonderful relationship with GOD now a great support system and I realized my heart needed counseling. I'm not ashamed to tell you my story. It's my TESTIMONY!!! This was not my only story of my life...but this was a part of my life that changed me forever. My heart will never bleed again because I allowed GOD to make me whole again. One day, GOD will send who he really has waiting on me. Until then. I will continue to let go of old chapter hurts, enjoy the new woman GOD is transforming me to be, live my best life as the Levite and example for my two Handsome boys. When you look at ME, you will never see Scars but my TESTIMONY is what I'm so proud of. If GOD saved ME!! He can Save you!

CHAPTER 7

Body Count Zero

"Surviving Cervical Cancer"

By: Tiffanie Davis Shelton

Buzzing around pollinating so many flowers, this is some crap! Life was happening and I was super busy, working a fulltime job as a nurse, being a fulltime caregiver for my disabled sister, losing my mother the year before and just starting school again. Being so preoccupied that I wasn't listening to my body screaming pay some attention to me!!!!

I started noticing my lower back bothered me more than usual. I ignored it, thinking I'm over worked or just using improper body mechanics on the job. Being a nurse, we often bypass our bladder's immediate needs to pee; so, I figured, this was a UTI or bladder infection. My thoughts were, I'll make myself an appointment soon. Then I started noticing blood on the tissue after I wiped along with increased spotting after intercourse! Well hell!! Why am I bleeding, and where is it coming from? If my tubes are tied and I haven't had a period in years.

I SUPPORT HER

I was concerned enough to make an appointment with the gynecologist. I've always kept my checkups for my pap smears so I wasn't too worried. I explained my concerns to the medical provider let's call her (Tina). Over the course of five office visits in four months, medical provider Tina was the only provider that performed the following VISUAL vaginal examine, obtained specimens from my vagina, sending me for an outpatient ultrasound and finally this procedure called LEEP (loop electrosurgical excision procedure) where they cut out abnormal tissue from your cervix and send it to the lab for testing.

I was thinking after five months what are you seeing now, that you didn't see five months ago! The next week I came in for a follow up from my procedure. "Medical provider (Tina), didn't seem to concern about my results she said "there was some abnormal cells but we would monitor them". As I was checking out to leave my appointment! Doctor (Frank Roberts), rushed to me out of nowhere and pleaded with me to come back to the exam room. He wanted to go over my results in depth! He read to me my results but all I heard was Squamous Cell Carcinoma.... I knew what that meant, I had Cancer! How was this (Mother Fucker) medical provider Tina going to let me walk out this office full of Cancer! I am devastated! I could've walked out of the doctor's office unaware of my diagnosis further delaying treatment. I could've been a *Body Count*"! A statistic! I wondered how many other women she was careless with! I couldn't be the only one.

The very next week I had my first consultation with the oncologist. Driving up to this building where cancer patients are treated gave me anxiety and an uneasy feeling! My thoughts were will I be alive this time next year, my son was serving overseas and my daughter lived in another state. I would need my babies to get through this journey and by the grace of God they came.

My sister Tamara, accompanied me to my first oncologist appointment. During this appointment your finances and insurance requirements are reviewed and then you see the doctor. The medical assistant took my vital signs and lead me to the exam room. I was asked to undress from the waist down, my palms were sweaty as I braced myself for the Oncologist to walk in to assess my situation and tell me how he was going to fix me. Even though I'm a nurse by profession, I'm a patient today and from here on out, tell it to me straight! Don't skip over nothing!

In comes Dr Bombay and two other people with him. His nurse and his scriber, taking down every word said. He had a great bedside manner and seemed to empathize with me. I was asked to lay down and scoot to the end of the table. During the examination small talk was made until Dr Bombay said "Oh, they didn't tell me you had a growth on your cervix"! My sister and I immediately turned and looked at each another in disbelief, imagining what was inside my vagina was a lot to process. I was scheduled for a Positron Emission Tomography (PET) scan which uses a radioactive substance called a trace to look for disease in the body. According to the scan it appeared the cancer had spread to my lymph nodes, after the exams and scans.

December 2014, right before Christmas, my first surgery was scheduled for January 2015. The doctor performed laparoscopic surgery where they extracted some of my lymph nodes and took a biopsy and verified the cancerous tumor was growing on my cervix and vaginal wall!

I was mentally preparing myself for what lies ahead. I have a fulltime job and I am fulltime caregiver for my sister Tonette. Once I got home and made my necessary phone calls to friends and family. I received an out pour of support from everyone. I'm about to literally fight to live! At my follow up appointment, Dr Bombay confirmed the cancer and it had not spread. We discussed the best treatment options for my particular Stage 2 Cervical Cancer. It was decided that I would have chemotherapy using the drug Cisplatin. This drug causes damage to your DNA, resulting in hair thinning, ringing of the ear, just to name a few. So, on Monday's for five weeks, I had to have radiation therapy Monday through Friday, after words I would also need a treatment called brachytherapy which is a procedure that uses a radioactive implant directly into the vagina. Most of my appointments I had someone with me, the morning of my first chemotherapy appointment I was so nervous, I didn't get much sleep the night before and I was very anxious. I walked into the building and checked into the area of the clinic where they did blood work on you prior to your chemotherapy appointment. If, all of your white blood count, platelets levels and hemoglobin come back within a normal range, you can keep your infusion appointment. So once my lab levels came back within normal limits, I was told to go to the second floor, the nurse took my vital signs and I was told I can sit in any of the recliners where they would access my chemo port and start my infusion with my chemotherapy drugs. They numb the access-port with lidocaine and I braced myself for the needle stick that they pushed into my chest, I cringed from the popping sound from the needle as the nurse access my chemo port. The nurse will tell you the name of every drug she is going to infuse, as well as verify your name and date of birth. During the first dose of chemotherapy running through my veins I felt cold and alone. I was thinking, I'm actually one of those people I saw on TV talking about how they lost their hair, and how depressed they were and how their life will never be the same again. I spoke with God most of the time during my infusion, it was like I was trying to make a deal with him. God, if I survive this cancer, I will help other survivors.

I looked around at all the other people getting their infusion and wondering what were they thinking? If they were thinking the same thing I was. My infusion lasted four hours from start to finish, the nurses were very nice and comforting. I met some nice people during my five-week treatments. Mondays were the long days for me I had both chemo and radiation therapy. By Wednesday, I felt so fatigued I barely had the stamina to hold myself up I never had any diarrhea which is one of the side effects I was told I may experience diarrhea I waited on it but my the grace of God it never came, and I was OK with that. I began l losing my appetite so they gave me Megace, it was an appetite stimulant. My taste buds no longer existed. The foods I once loved like fried crabs tasted horrible. Mostly everything tasted like metal. I also noticed my hair started to thinning on the top of my head. I was mentally getting prepared to lose my hair. The more I looked at myself in the mirror she wasn't me anymore. I was very critical of myself I didn't feel pretty anymore. I was too tired to put in the energy into caring for myself. My only thought was surviving. I was surprised to learn that there really wasn't too much community information about cervical cancer. Not the way the information is readily available for breast cancer. My second week of chemo I started noticing changes in my bowels. My radiation appointments consisted of, coming and checking into at the reception desk swiping my card only to go back into the waiting area with the other cancer patients waiting to get **FRIED!**

When it was my turn, I laid on the table while they marked my body with a marker. They do this in order to concentrate on the area of the tumor. From that experience I started noticing my vaginal area becoming swollen and tender. I discussed my symptoms with the radiation doctor, she prescribed me a regimen that had to be mixed up at the pharmacy then I would apply it to my vagina. When I started using this medication it made me ill to my stomach, the smell of the medicines that they mix together to help soothe the affected area smelled like a combination of burning flesh and medicine. I laid down to take a nap every chance I got, trying to rest my body for the next day and radiation.

My skin wouldn't hold moisture anymore. I became more conscious of the ingredients of everything I put on my skin. I purchased all kinds of creams and extra moisturizing lotions. My skin seemed to soak up everything I apply. Even the lotions that the doctors recommended had chemicals in it. I started thinking about what can I use on my body that was chemical free so I started researching natural products to see what there ingredients were. I thought to myself, I can do this once I get well! I'm going to make my own natural products for people in my situation. During my five weeks of chemo I had a major event happen to where I had to skip a week of treatment. Sadly, I lost my father during this time. He was one of my greatest supporters, he would accompany me on my appointments and would sacrifices his lunchtime to come support me. It was very hard to continue treatment after you lose a parent at such a very vulnerable time in your life. I was sad a lot thinking about him. It was completely unexpected. My aunt Barbara, stepped in as a parent. We leaned on her for everything at that time. She helped me with my sister

Tonette, seeing Aunt Barbara show up to the house brighten my day. We talked about everything!

I needed support so I made up my mind when I finished all of my treatments, I was going to Oklahoma on a little vacation to visit my daughter Kierstin and her family. During my last week of treatment, I just didn't feel like Tiffanie. I knew the chemo drug ravished the good cells as well as the cancerous cells. I had to be careful around people with colds and wear a mask so I wouldn't get sick. I have a procedure coming up called Brachytherapy which involves placing radioactive material inside of your body in my case my vagina. Internal radiation was needed as my last treatment to make sure the tumor shrunk. This required me to stay overnight at the hospital where I would undergo four treatments and 24 hours of my hospital stay. This will be the first time getting an epidural in my back. I was put to sleep for this procedure. I woke up with this contraption in my vagina it was very un-comfortable. My bed was at a 30° semi Fowler's position. I wasn't sitting up enough to eat a meal if I wanted to. I was wheeled down at the appointed time to the radiation department with my legs up in stirrups and I received radiation in that manner. During the course of the evening my left side became flaccid it felt like wobbly Jell-O I couldn't feel my body I had no control of the left side of my body. I push the call button for the nurse in a panic the nurse came in I told them what was going on and they immediately called for the anesthesiologist. The anesthesiologist came to my room and assessed me. He adjusted the medication and my body started to come back to life. Little did I know that little mishap will cause trouble for me later on. I was discharged from the hospital the next morning. I was tired and fatigued mentally and physically. I was looking forward to traveling and spending some time with one of my kids. Once I arrived in Oklahoma I could relax and take my mind off of the events that have taken place weeks prior. I enjoyed myself with my daughter son-in-law and grandchildren. The plan was to stay a week or a little more. I noticed I wasn't using the bathroom it actually became a task a hard task at that. It was concerning enough for me to go to the emergency room. The ER physician recommended that I take a laxative and I should be good to go. Well that wasn't the case. I started feeling worse as the days went by to where I had to cut my trip short and get back to see my doctor I knew something wasn't right. I booked an appointment with my radiation doctor and they saw that I had stool built up in my colon. She gave me a prescription for Dulcolax. Me thinking as a nurse made myself a concoction so I could shit! Lord add to their concoction and my stomach started spasming like crazy to the point where I was on my tippy toes. I had my niece drive me to the ER not knowing I wouldn't be out of here for 45 days. The first few days in the hospital the doctors were trying to figure out what was going on with my colon. I was scheduled for a colonoscopy hoping that will give me the answers that I needed. I went for the procedure and woke up to the doctor telling me he couldn't get the camera up my ass. And I would need exploratory surgery. The whole time I'm thinking what in the world is going on with me now. I prepared for another procedure; I met my surgeon Dr. Joe he told me based off of what he saw on the x-ray's but he couldn't guarantee that I wouldn't wake up without a colostomy bag on. I wasn't sure if I heard him right I couldn't imagine what he was talking about not for me I just finished cancer treatment. All I know is I needed to use the bathroom And the doctor had to figure it out. Low and behold when I woke up I had a colostomy bag. Dr. Joe said my colon was black and hard as a brick and he needed to allow it to relax and heal up before he can try and fix it. Apparently, I was so jacked up, there was another surgeon on board a urologist due to my kidneys being swollen to the point where I needed ureteral stents to help my urine flow! Ugh! To make matters worse I already was feeling bad and not feeling attractive. Now I had this shit bag on my stomach for GOD knows how long I was in a funk figuratively speaking. I prayed about it and tried to be positive, after all I was alive! I spent all of June, 2015 in the hospital; my summer had started off rotten. I had to learn how to care for my colostomy bag, how to change it, how to look for signs and symptoms of infection. I also had to learn what to do if there was no poo coming out. It was tough trying to get used to not being able to use the core of my body, we take our health for granted! I was obsessed with looking at myself in the mirror naked staring at this colostomy bag I couldn't get over it but I knew I had to get through it. My body has gone through so many changes within six months. I still have many follow-up appointments scheduled. I also started having left-sided weakness from the radiation to which I started physical therapy. I could hardly lift my legs up to put them in the car to drive I was so weak from the treatments and having major surgeries back to back. My body had no time to recover.

I started feeling sorry for myself, I cried I was missing my mother I needed my mama, but I pressed through and got through my appointments.

As the holidays were approaching, I wanted to celebrate everyone who took the time out to support me in anyway during my journey. I came up with the idea of renting a beach house for the Christmas holiday week. I wanted to have my children and grandchildren here with me. We could have a big family gathering and I can do a brunch for my support system as a kind gesture to say thank you for everything. I ran the idea by my sister Tamara, she organized the festivities as to what we had planned on a daily basis. I sent out mass text messages to see which family members and friends will be able to participate it was like a mini family reunion. Family from Detroit, Oklahoma and Florida came to celebrate. My current coworkers and pass coworkers came out for my brunch the Sunday before Christmas. My childhood friends that I continue to keep in touch with some of whom I've known for over 40 something years, the outpouring love was awesome. This celebration took my mind off of my worries for a little bit I needed it. All was well until I ate a little bit too much of an edible sent down by my kids father. I didn't realize everyone else maybe eat a half a brownie with the weed in it, the brownies were so good, I ate a whole one. I was due to pick up my mother-in-law from the airport she was flying in from Michigan to spend some time out at the beach house with us. I was driving along headed towards the airport and I suddenly started feeling hot all over, I have an urge to strip, I couldn't control it. I knew something was going on with me I didn't feel like normal. I realized I was having a reaction from the edible. "Laud I was Trippin" I can laugh about it now but at the time that shit wasn't funny at all! I stopped at the nearest 7-Eleven and walked in and asked these people could they call 911 then I ran back out to my car. I started taking off my clothes but I was trying to control my thoughts and make myself keep them on. I was feeling hot and anxious I was climbing in the seat of my car. I started becoming paranoid and my head felt like it was swimming. I started praying and calling on the Lord like no other. The paramedics finally arrived I tried to explain to them what had happened but somehow another day ended up strap me down like I was crazy. We arrived at the hospital and I heard them say she ate something with drugs in it. My family arrived at the hospital and my sister tried to explain that I had a brownie laced with weed or something in it. I was hooked up to all these monitors in the ER. My heart monitor was racing from 125 to 130 and I was hollering somebody help me at the top of my lungs for over an hour. It seemed like they put me off in a corner room somewhere until the effects wore off. The nurse finally came in with an Ativan injection thank you God! I was kept overnight for observation. The next day I was discharged and I headed back to the beach house. My family welcomed me back with jokes of course. That was an ordeal in itself I couldn't believe that happened to me. Everyone else enjoyed the edible in moderation. I think I was the only one who ate a whole brownie. Never again!...

Shortly after the holidays the new year was approaching 2016 January. Keep in mind I was going to my oncology checkup and gastroenterologist surgeon Dr. Joe had discussed the things I needed to do in order to have my colostomy bag reversed. One of the options to ensure a successful surgery, was for me to go into the hyperbaric oxygen chamber, which helps in wound healing by supplying oxygen to damaged tissue so once he tried to re-attach my colon and rectum back together it will be a success. Keep in mind I have not pooped in almost a year out of my rectum. I was scheduled for maybe thirty hyperbaric chamber appointments which were about two hours every day except weekends. I wasn't a fan of being closed into a tight space but if this was going to help me get back to myself, I was willing to try it. Once you get there you were not to have on any lotions, perfumes and powders or anything of that nature. You went into a dressing room and undressed and put it in a hospital gown. I got on the hospital bed and was pushed into this skinny glass tube like a capsule once you're in there you couldn't sit up, if you bend your knees you would be a few inches away from the top of the machine. Before the door closes I started swallowing so my ears could sustain the pressure from the oxygen chamber. I could handle the first twenty-five treatments but on the twenty-six treatment I had a panic attack and once I was in the chamber for maybe ten minutes, I hit the button for them to let me out that was the end for me I've had enough! I contacted my surgeon's office to let them know that my treatments were finished and I want to be scheduled to have my colostomy bag reversed as soon as possible. All the necessary pre-surgery testing has been done and I was preparing for my colostomy reversal. Dr. Joe did inform me that I will be losing part of my colon due to bowel necrosis and that he would be reattaching a healthy organ the remaining colon to a radiated organ the rectum. The risk would be I wouldn't be able to control my bowels. I was willing to take that chance. This was a happy day for me I couldn't wait to get back to normal. Praying and thanking God for getting me through this uncertain time in my life. I often thought about was this all worth it! This whole experience was horrible. Even with the support, you feel alone because it is you with the diagnosis. I had cancer went, through the treatment, the treatment caused me to have all these other medical issues. My faith has kept me going all this time and the support from friends and family. That was an instrumental part in my healing and recovery. Needless to say, my surgery went well I'm on the road to recovery mentally emotionally physically. I have been out of work for year and a half, and I started back working October 2016. I started brainstorming about the business I wanted to start and how I could be a blessing and get the message out that cancer doesn't have to be a death sentence. For at least a year the thought of what I wanted to do for a business played out in my head but there was no action behind it yet. I was concentrating on what I wanted to educate the community about Cervical Cancer. I was coming out of the darkness into the light. I gather information and educational materials; January is cervical cancer awareness month so I wanted to have an educational awareness event in January 2017. A good friend of mine Angela Stucky. who owns a beauty salon in Chesapeake Virginia called Shadez of Beauty; was gracious enough to allow me to have my first event at her business. As women it is imperative that we do get our annual pap smears as well as our mammograms. We need to listen to our bodies and stop ignoring the signals and be proactive about our health. Signs and symptoms aren't always going to be worse case scenario but you have to get in to see your physician and not keep putting it off. I feel even though I went through all that I did that I was fortunate. I could've walked out of the doctor's office and not shown back up for six months later who knows and have a different prognosis. As I started feeling better and getting acclimated back to work, I paced myself to regain my stamina and change the way I was eating. I started to do a little research towards the business I wanted to create. I knew I wanted to do something involving natural skin care without the chemicals. I came up with the name for my business called Teal Box Cosmetics. Teal represents "cervical cancer" and the box is where the cancer was present in my vagina. I had the opportunity to partake in a community shark event on my birthday April 27, 2019 at the "Something in the Water music festival". I pitched my business idea to a panel of judges and I was selected as one of the five prize winners. Winning this prize money really meant a lot and this gave me the motivation to go full force with my business along with the help and guidance from my business coach and friend Danielle Ferreira who made my vision come to life.

My purpose is to use my platform to give back to the community, educate and bring awareness to other women and perhaps help them through their journey because all of our journeys are not the same. Sometimes we are pushed into our purpose by tragedy I would often say Lord if you get me out of this one. I would use my journey for good. I had to visualize my survival in my mind before it was possible. I didn't know who I was until I went through this journey and discovered a me, I didn't know existed. God is faithful, don't let the lack of evidence convince you nothing is happening. I am a five-year cancer survivor now. This did not come without some residual medical issues following my colostomy reversal, I had to go in a few times for an outpatient colorectal dilatation where they inflate the balloon attached to catheter to stretch my bowel. This had to be done because of the narrowing of my stools. If that wasn't bad enough, the side effects from the brachytherapy narrows and shortened your vaginal canal. So, if you don't use it, you lose it! Yikes! The radiation oncologist always took her time and gave it to me straight no chaser. If you don't have a Boo to screw, you will need to use this dilator to keep your vagina flexible. I'm thinking all of this could shut my sex life down for good! Easing back into intimacy had its challenging my first experience after my recovery was with a prominent Naval Officer who was no strangers to me. If you have an understanding mature partner who cares what's going on with you and takes their time sex will be enjoyable again. The only good thing about this experience was the weight loss. I got down to 139 pounds. I was nice size but I had no energy and my I felt like the wind could blow me down. Plus, I was still recovering from previous surgery. Once my food started to reabsorb again, I looked healthy real fast. My sugar cravings stayed away for a while and I was able to maintain a decent weight. Aside from that feeding myself with positive literature and focusing on self-care. Having a different attitude towards life. Reflecting on the kind words spoken to me by a stranger. I wonder why it's easier to tell a stranger all your business. This stranger sat beside me sometimes during chemo. The first time I saw her I noticed she talks a lot and I was glad she was on the other side of the room because I like closing my eyes to think during this four-hour long infusion. The following week the only open chair was next to her. She sat quite for a little bit then we struck up a conversation. We talked the whole time. Her infusion time was over before mine but before she left, she handed me this Angel she made, today was her last treatment day. She gave me a hug and said Tiffanie, you are going to make it out of here don't worry. I never saw her again and I kept that angel. I believed God positioned her to talk with me. She was also a vital part of my support system.

My sisters, if you are reading my story and you have been recently diagnosed with cancer or knows someone who has please know that you are not alone. There are resources available that can help you such as the National Cervical Cancer Coalition "NCCC", in which I utilized for my recovery and support. Remember to never be afraid to tell your story, speak your truth, not only will it save your life but it may help to save the life of someone else.

CHAPTER 8

Beauty For Ashes

"Recovery from Childhood Trauma"

By: Tyishua McCoy

Have you ever met a woman who was so beautiful and vibrant, they looked like they had it all together, not a thing out of place? When you would see her, she always had a warm and beautiful sincere smile on her face, make-up flawless, even without make-up, she was still very enchanting. Everyone she met loved her, and was drawn to her energy, her light and the aura she possessed. She walked as if she stood 10 ft. tall and full of confidence. She was not just intelligent, she was educated, street and book smart. This woman could walk in any room, fill it with the sweet aroma of her persona; mixed with charm and humility. Everyone looked and paid attention to the class, grace and elegance she represented. The looks and stares she received were not just of jealously or envy but, more of admiration and respect. This was the type of woman, that any man, "a real gentleman", could see greatness with in his life. A woman with a nurturing spirit that held a little mystery. This woman holds the elegance and class of Diahann Carroll and the stunning beauty of Dorothy Dandridge. Now, without a doubt, these types of women exist, because my grandmother was this woman, my mother was this woman, I am this woman!

The journey that you are about to take, will be one of love, laughter, joy, pain, heartbreak, disappointment, tragedy and triumph. This young teenage girl who grew up too fast through her own experiences with rape, teen pregnancies, substance abuse, AIDS, bullying, depression, homelessness, and judicial issues, all while trying to discover her true purpose in life. Feelings of emptiness and shame that haunted everyday then, and some of those situations that still haunt her today.

My mother was 22 years old when she gave birth to me. I was born May 23rd, 1973 to Mrs. Brenda Louise King-Greene. My mother had gotten married right out of high school. She told me she did that because, she wanted to be on her own, and be with the man she thought she loved, and who loved her. She wanted to live her life the way she wanted to live it. No, this man was not my father! As a matter of fact, I had never met the man she had married, and my mother just happened to still be married, but separated, when she met my father. She eventually divorced Mr. Greene, but she was no longer in a relationship with my father either when I was born. My mother didn't even want him to know I existed. My dad must have hurt my mother pretty bad for her to go to that extreme.

Now, why do I mention this? Think about how powerful words and actions are! The very things we speak into our lives, and the lives of our children play a huge part in our upbringing and in our future

I SUPPORT HER

Generational curses are real!

Why, as women, do we feel that when a man has emotionally, or mentally wounded us, we should do more things to cause ourselves even more harm and pain? Like, keep them away from the kids, not accept any financial assistance, basically, sabotage all relationships that come after him, or just simply not forgive him, or ourselves for what has happened past or present! As parents, do we really think about the things that we do or say around our children? Certain conversations we may have, people we choose to be around or incorporate in our lives, or places we may go or frequent that as parents, we probably shouldn't be a part of or around. Growing up as an only child with a single mom who looked like a super star, at least I thought so, was the greatest thing ever. She was so classy, everywhere we went people would stare, and say how beautiful she was.

I would play in her clothes, perfume, jewelry, shoes and of course her make-up. You would think because she was single that she had men lined up around the corner, I am sure she did, however, this was not the life she presented in front of me. From all that knew her friends and family, they say she truly carried herself as one classy lady. My mom stood 6' feet tall flat footed, she was truly beautiful. She was always very well dressed, with her own since of style and fashion so elegantly different, she was also a local model in the Hampton Roads area for a local optometrist she worked for, for several years. While modeling the stylish eyeglasses that were sold in his establishment, she also studied Ophthalmology at Norfolk State University. She had her own hopes and dreams of becoming an optometrist. My mom had this gazillion dollar smile that would brighten anybody's day, or any room she entered. She had a laugh that was so infectious, you knew when she was present. My mom was that friend, sister, and auntie everybody wanted to be around.

As I was growing up, other than my father, I saw only three men in my mom's life; that she bought around me. Now, if there were others, I didn't see them. But, the three men that I saw, my mom probably didn't know this, but I knew their first and last name and what they did and where they worked. I heard and watched everything! If you are a parent, trust me, your children watch and hear everything! If they see it or hear it, they have absorbed whatever it was in some form or fashion. Out of the three men, there was only one that would change the life of my mother and me. This would be the last man that I would know my mother to love, and impact her life as well as mine, this would be Mr. Fred Glen. She really loved him, because the next thing I knew, he was moving in with us. By this time, I had to be around seven years old. Up until now it was only mommy and me, and now Mr. Fred makes three! Do we really understand, that as mothers or fathers, how our children are impacted by the things we allow them to see! As parents, whatever we are experiencing, whether it's good, bad or indifferent, our children are experiencing those things right along with us. Sometimes our actions and the actions of our parents or those that took care of us, can directly or indirectly effect or affect us in some way by past or current events. No matter how much our parents tried, or how much we try to protect our children now, the inevitable is and will happen. Parenting doesn't come with a manual, or self-help videos. We can only provide our children with the tools and the knowledge we were given along with past experiences we had as children growing up. When I look back, I definitely see things my mom did back then that I currently mimic now, and I mean like "Damn mirror!" After Fred moved in, of course, I was a little jealous and I felt like I was losing my mom. Not because she wasn't paying me any attention, because, now I had to share her with someone. I'm sure every now and again some kid feels like this when someone new enters the home outside of the biological parent that may be absent, or even when a new sibling come into the picture. The dynamics change! I don't think he knew how to form a relationship with me. But the real question is; did he want one? Did my mom want there to be one? She kept a certain amount of distance between Fred and me. I wonder if she even knew how to bring us all together to be a family. My mom came from a home that had both parents present, married, sharing and living in a home with only the children they raised. I think this may have been very unfamiliar territory for her, as it is for many families today. She may have not known how to bridge that family gap between her daughter and a man that she knew was not my father.

My mother was happy, very happy! She had love in her life, and she still was the fun mom, the go to the beach mom, the drive-in movies mom, the pack a lunch let's go to the concert in the park mom, the let's go see a show mom! My mom knew I loved music; she filled our place with so much of it. She heard me sing an Angela Bofield song that she played on repeat all the time in the house, it was called "Tonight I Give In" and she lit up like a Christmas tree when she heard me hit these notes! My mom would always say, "I couldn't carry a tune if it was in a bucket. But you, little girl, you got something!" She was on a mission to show off her little girl to the world. She took me to every show that hit Hampton Roads. I have seen so many live performances, from Luther Vandross, Whitney Houston, Atlantic Starr, Kool and the Gang, Michael Jackson and the Jackson 5, and many more. We would go to operas, and plays, I mean the list goes on and on. She wanted me to imagine myself on these same platforms, she wanted that image to be a vision in my mind daily. She made sure I maintained my weight, by keeping me actively involved in ballet, tap dance, baton, and trips to the YMCA for swimming classes. I was a busy little girl! My mom wanted to make sure I well versed and cultured, she would send me to different camps and workshops during the summer time. She wanted to make certain I had no kind of self-esteem issues. She involved me in modeling schools, etiquette classes, pageants, and anything to do with singing, from the church choir, to local talent shows at school or within the community were to say the least. She wanted me there front and center, comfortable and confident! Around this time, I was in the 2nd grade, and my grades were not at their best. When she saw I was struggling in school, she thought it was because she had me involved in too many things, so she quickly got me help. I had tutors after school and even a child psychologist, which led to her finding out that I had a learning disorder. Dyslexia! If you are not familiar with this disorder, in simple terms, dyslexia is a learning disability that makes it difficult to read, write, and spell in spite of normal intelligence and adequate instruction. It is caused by the brain's inability to process information received from the eyes or ears into understandable language. It does not mean that the child is lazy, or not trying hard, or not intelligent. It just means that they need to be taught in a different way. There are several types of this learning disorder, mine was associated with Left Right Confusion. I was left-handed, and would constantly transpose letter and numbers.

This disorder can be treated, but there is no cure. However, back in August of 2000, The American Psychological Association, an American scientist has gathered new evidence on the link between left-handedness and intellectual creativity, confirming that "true left-handers" tend to be more intelligent and eloquent than right handers, and better at solving problems. Just thought I would throw that out there to all my left-handed counterparts! With this new discovery, my mom was determined to push me no matter what. She was not going to feel sorry for me, or let me use it as an excuse to feel sorry for myself. I definitely had my issues in school, I sometimes felt like the big dumb kid, because I was taller than everybody in the class and I wasn't a skinny kid either, I was quite curvy for a little girl and I was just not as quick with the assignments as everyone, but by the time I got to the 5th grade I didn't struggle as much, and I knew when and how to ask for help at this point, but for some reason I still always felt different. Of course, I couldn't help but wonder why my mom's boyfriend, Mr. Fred was never a part of these events concerning me. I used to think, maybe he didn't care or want to be involved because he wasn't my dad, or did my mom even want him to be a part of those activities. However, my mom made sure, he was good no matter what, and I never felt as if she wasn't there for me. I watched how she treated this man and how he treated her, as far as I could see, they were good and she was happy. Between my grandparents, and my mom and Fred these were the only true blueprints and examples of relationship that would set me up to be the woman, wife, and mother I am today. I would like to reflect on a very important matter here. To all my ladies and gentlemen that are married, single, divorced, or living with your significant others, and you have children from a previous relationship, please take the time to reflect on those situations and how they impact children in blended family relationships. If you are keeping those relationships from flourishing, everyone involved could be missing out on a wonderful opportunity to learn new thing, to incorporate and experience more love, patience, kindness, and the ability to have more family included in the building of the relationship within the home. This mindset would also assist with the parent that is absent, or not there on a daily basis.

I SUPPORT HER

I honestly feel there was an injustice done, because Fred was not a part of those milestones in my life, whether my biological father was in my life or not, he was the man in the household, and I had no consistent presence of my own father, and we both could have benefited from the relationship. If my mother trusted him enough to be with us in the home, why not incorporate everyone as a family. But, again, not sure why there was so much separation within the household.

Where is my father you ask? We will bring him in a little later. At this point life seemed to be really good. My mom was working a lot and I was starting to see less of her. She was going to a lot of house parties, and some I was even right there with her. There were a lot of parties at our house to. Now, Fred definitely participated in those activities. We were not attending church or going to Granny's house as much either. And the next thing I know, my Mom springs it on me that we are moving! I'm thinking maybe it's because Fred proposed, and they are getting married, or they bought a house together, because we did live in an apartment even though it was a really nice place, it still was an apartment. But when she said she got a new job, and she wanted to move closer to the job, I was devastated! In my head, I am thinking, like, we have a car, it's not like you have to catch the bus or walk like we used to, I mean it was a two-hour bus ride from the Oceanfront to Downtown, Norfolk.

Things changed very drastically, and life as I knew it would never be the same again! So, we moved in this two-bedroom apartment that was the size of our living room at the last apartment. I couldn't even have my same bedroom furniture. Only a day bed or twin bed would fit in my room and one bathroom! I hated it! I wasn't sure what happened to all of our furniture. I guess it was in storage or she sold it. If she got a new job, why are we moving to something that was smaller than what we had before, something just didn't seem right.

I had to leave all my friends and my school. Now, most of my friends were white and so was the school I attended, I had a few black friends and it was a pretty nice neighborhood and school. I never got into any trouble or fights and things were pretty cool. There were plenty of playgrounds, a pool and a clubhouse that we could go to in the summer time. I could even ride my bike to the beach.

The neighborhood we moved to was drug infested and full of kids that looked like me, I mean all black, no white people in sight in my neighborhood and only a few in my school. However, my cousins and my aunt and uncle all lived in close proximity of each other. I loved growing up with my cousins close to me. Being an only child had its moments of loneliness. In Virginia Beach, we had the same set up where we all lived close together. My aunt and uncle actually moved to this neighborhood first. Why? I am not sure. But I am a kid, so my feelings didn't matter and I didn't have a say in any of this. The only friends I had at this point were my cousins. I guess that was the big plus. I could cruise on over to my cousins' place, just like when we lived at the Oceanfront.

Now we are starting to settle in, and I am having a really tough time adjusting. However, mom and Fred started fighting a lot. Sometimes he was there, sometimes he wasn't. I didn't know what was going on. I honestly didn't care because, trust me, I had my own problems to deal with! The girls hated me, and the boys paid too much attention to me. When we moved, I was already in the 6th grade. My first day of school was horrible. Again, I was the tallest girl in school, and so I stood out like an orange on an apple tree. Every girl in the neighborhood seemed to be in a clique and I did not fit in anywhere. One day in school a boy spoke to me during lunch. He just asked my name and where I was from. By the end of the day after school, a group of girls were waiting in my court with sticks, bats, and chains ready to fight me behind a boy who just asked me my name! Apparently, this was the norm in this neighborhood, so I tried to stay to myself, or just sit in front of my door. There was a brother and sister that lived in the same court as me. His name was Eugene and his sister's name was Chamira. They were always nice to me, they would speak every day, and her brother always was doing something funny or silly to make me laugh. There was another young girl who lived two doors down, named Tina. She was pregnant, but I knew she was not that old, because I saw her catching a school bus. As I started to hang out a little bit more, I would meet others in the neighborhood. I had girls and boys who were always picking on me, spreading rumors, or who wanted to fight for whatever reason they would make up in their head. I just didn't understand. Why are they picking on me? Why are they calling me names? Why are they so cruel?

I would come home and tell my mom, and all I got was "They are jealous of you." I am like. "Jealous of what? We all live in the same place, go to the same school, and probably going through some of the same situations at home. What is it that makes someone jealous of that!" My mom said, "No, baby, you are different. You will always, in some way, experience this throughout life – now, and as you become an adult. And there is nothing wrong with being different." I said, "Momma, they joke the way I look, talk, and dress. They say I talk to proper or I sound white, and I always wore dresses or skirts. What am I, a religious freak or something?" My mom said you don't always were dresses, you have worn pants, jeans and shorts, I just prefer you in dresses and skirts, because you are a lady! Point blank. I got tired of all this bullying and name calling. I wanted to be liked, I wanted friends. The girls really hated me and the boys...well let's just say...I didn't stand a chance in hell of getting a boyfriend, not in that neighborhood, because some girl somewhere was going to drag my name through the mud if she thought a boy was looking my way, especially if she low-key liked him. I couldn't even talk to a boy without someone automatically thinking that we were having sex! Middle school was the worst. And with all the joking, bullying and name calling and rumors, and fighting, I just was at my lowest point. The rumors were just as off the chain as all the other stuff I was experiencing. I had some terrible awful things said about me, behind my back and up close in my face. I knew I was different from the other kids. Different in how I acted, talked, looked, and thought, this was very apparent. Because what I really wanted to do was punch all of them in the face, and spread a couple of rumors and some truths of my own. I wanted them to hurt like I hurt, feel like I felt. I never admitted it or said it out loud, I just kept it bottled up on the inside but, it was my reality.

I remember the first time I heard someone say I was ugly, or that I looked like a monkey! I had never heard someone say such awful things about a person, or about me. I have heard the too tall jokes, but never to this degree, until I was around people who were the same complexion as me, kids who mothers and grandmothers looked like mine. You know our parents and family members really be setting us up for the okie-doke. They always telling us how beautiful or handsome we are as children, never telling us that someone, somewhere will think the total opposite of this visual they have of us. From there, the insults just got worst, it went from one extreme to the next. They called me Donkey Kong, Grape-ape, to Magilla Gorilla! I remember how I felt the first time I heard those words describing me. It was like a great shame that hovered over me, those words pierced through me like someone had took a dagger to my chest, twisted it and pulled it out and then poured salt and alcohol on it. I had not done a thing to these kids. I didn't really have any come backs or jokes to say back at them. I wasn't that quick with my delivery of insults, because this wasn't something I had ever experienced. Our parents never let us joke each other, we couldn't call each other names, other than the ones we were born with. Hell, we couldn't even do nick names! But the ultimate situation took place that would change me forever. The kids got on the bus one day, with a boom box playing the song, Brass Monkey, yep the old Beastie Boys tune, and while they were singing it loud and proud, they began to throw banana peels at me. This broke me down to a place, I thought surely, I would never recover from. How could I ever walk around with any dignity? How could I ever feel good about myself? I had people who didn't even want to be friends with me in fear of catching this negative attention towards them.

    I couldn't understand why these kids were so cruel and hateful towards me. I wasn't nasty or weird looking, I didn't stink, I dressed fairly decent, and I was polite and friendly to everyone. I just wanted to be liked. I cried every day to my mom! She thought I was exaggerating, until one morning I ran back in the house crying because a girl pulled a razor on me at the bus stop… for no reason! The girl with the razor just kept saying, I know you was talking about me. I am trying to figure out who in the hell she was, because I would have to know you in order to talk about you. She didn't catch the bus at our stop. Her sole purpose was to be there to agitate me. The girl ran up and tried to cut me, and I went to kick the razor out her hand and I ripped my skirt! The other kids at the bus stop just laughed as I ran off. I ran into the house crying, scared, and embarrassed and told my mom what happened. Now, when I say this got my mom so heated she ran outside in her robe and slippers, waved the bus driver down to stop the bus, she hopped on, and screamed out...what is wrong with you people, you out here acting like a bunch of damn animals! I knew after that...I was really in for it. This definitely prompted my mom to go to the school. She wanted to talk with someone about the treatment I was receiving, because honestly, bullying had not really made a serious enough impact for schools to address it as a problem, nor was it a great concern to some parents. My mom could have talked until she was blue in the face, but there was nothing that she or the school could have done to solve this problem that I was having. Just know that day, when I got home, someone had egged our front door and windows. At this point I just wanted to die. A hate brewed inside of me so strong that I wanted to do nothing but seek revenge. I wanted to get them all back. Somehow, someway, one day. For days I was depressed, and very distantly even contemplated thoughts of suicide. I didn't have much to say, but several different thoughts were running through my head as to what I was feeling. Do I fight back? Do I become what they say I am? Do I kill them or plant the same fear in them that they planted in me? I needed help, and clearly this was unfamiliar territory for me. Why would God allow these people to treat me like this!

At this point, I said if I can't beat em, join em! I was going to make sure they knew my name, since it was thrown under the bus and dragged through the mud anyway. Why not give them something to talk about! I used all the talents and gifts that I was born with and even a few that I even learned from the hostile treatment. I became a cheerleader, I played basketball, volleyball, and I ran track. I loved being involved in extracurricular activities, because I was able to meet new people from other cities and schools. I thought for sure this was a better way to meet new people who didn't know me. But the people I lived around were determined to destroy me. BUT WHY? Why was I going through this? What did I do to deserve this? Why did we move here? Why was God punishing me? Now, when I look back, I see there were specific reasons for me to go through these experiences of being broken down verbally, mentally, physically, emotionally, and spiritually.

In this day and time most people do not have good coping skills. Trust me, it is a learned behavior. In order to even endure certain types of situations, you must be able to cope! I didn't have very many friends back then but the few I had were pretty cool to hang out with. Two of the girls who I hung tight with was, Candice, she was also on my cheering squad, and Crystal, she was a little older and was in high school but we met while hanging out in the neighborhood. These young ladies were beautiful, fun, and full of life. I was taught not to be jealous of anything or anyone! I know without a doubt, I carried myself like this, and I am sure this was intimidating to some and baffling to many. It was a big thing back then for girls to compare themselves and hate on each other, and for the boys, it was game. Because I was so broken from the words that had been thrown at me everyday, I couldn't help but to think, "Am I really this ugly person, that nobody would want to talk to, hang around, or even associate with in any kind of way?" When I say no matter where I was or where I would go, it seemed that I couldn't catch a break. I was not big on fighting, but this place definitely turned me into one tough sista. As time went on, I saw myself slowly changing into someone else. I was talking different, I saw myself doing and saying things, I was not supposed to do or say, and honestly, I didn't really want to do these things, but I was in survival mode. My mom and Fred were arguing more and I didn't understand why or what was going on but things seem to be getting worse between them, and one day my world was turned upside down. I heard them arguing and I over heard him say something about her sniffing white power up her nose! I thought I was hearing things. My heart had dropped down to my stomach, there was no way that this was happening. I was praying to God that this was not true! One day while we were on our way to the grocery store, she had asked me to get something out of the glove box, and to my surprise I saw this little small container that had some white powder in it. This scared me to death. From everything that you see and hear on TV, and the movies, and in school, I knew that it was something that was very bad. I didn't know how long she had been using, but I knew that it had to be a problem, because the next thing I know she was going into a rehabilitation facility. She wasn't there long, and Fred was on his way out. The relationship had become so toxic with his drinking and her drugging, he in fact left, and my mother definitely was on her way to a downward spiral. With my mother really no longer concerned about what I was doing or where I was going, I found myself drifting further and further away from being this teenage girl to becoming a young woman, who now had to figure it out and take care of herself.

My mother no longer looked the same. She was hanging around different people, coming in and out the apartment. I saw this situation getting worse, and so was the situation with me, because now I knew, along with the whole neighborhood, that my mom was smoking crack! I knew exactly what it was and there were so many people in the neighborhood that were selling it, or either using it right in the front of your face! I definitely was scared of the unknown. When I say this drug will have you doing the craziest shit, I mean, some things had me terrified to be in the same house with her, or anybody that did this drug. There were so many times that I would come in the house and my mom would have all the mirrors in the house covered with sheets! One time I found her in a tub full of ice water talking to herself. I didn't understand what was happening to her or what was going on. There were times I came home and there was no food, nothing but a jug of milk or water in the refrigerator but every now and again, somehow, she had something prepared.

The year is 1989, and this drug had completely taken over our lives. I'm seeing myself change so much, I felt lost. By now, everyone in the neighborhood knows that my mother is on drugs. She's hanging with other crackheads and she's buying from local drug dealers. Some right in the same neighborhood. At this point I no longer wanted to be around her, live in this house, or be in this neighborhood. It was just so embarrassing and I felt so ashamed. There were no more family members close for me to go to and wait it out while my mother would go on these binges. Sometimes, I didn't know if she was dead or alive. There was a period of time that my mother was dealing with people within the neighborhood who were local drug dealers, some seemed to be not much older than me. On a few occasions, they would be in the house when I would come home. One in particular, she was arguing with in front of me and it definitely seemed to be about some money being owed. A few weeks later I found myself face down in the dirt a few steps away from my own house being raped and beaten by someone who seemed to be very familiar with who I was...they called me by name as I was knocked unconscious, and when I came to, I felt as if a ton of bricks had fallen on top of me, ripped from the inside out, and when I finally made it home no one was there! Complete silence. This was it was for me I wanted to be anywhere but here. I even left for a while to stay with my aunt for a while to live in a different neighborhood and go to a different school, only to end up experiencing the same things.

A few months later I found out I was pregnant. Scared and terrified, I had to tell my mom because I wanted to go live with my dad. Even though I knew who my dad was, and he lived in the same state as me, he could have taken me out of this situation. He was not there on a consistent basis; however, my mother never spoke an ill, or disrespectful word about my dad around me. As far as I knew, they had a great relationship. So why didn't he come to my rescue? Of course, my mom told my dad. My dad asked who got me pregnant, and funny how I was more horrified to tell them I was raped than blurting out some random boy's name. My dad told my mom I had to get an abortion! At the time, I was not on my dad's insurance, so being I was going to live with him, he had to add me. By the time my dad's girlfriend, Louise, took me to the clinic they told me they could no longer do the procedure; I was already 8 weeks! As I laid there crying and screaming in Louise's arms, I felt so hopeless. What was I going to do with a baby? But Louise took care of everything – she signed me up for school, got me Medicaid, WIC, and found me an obstetrician. I had not seen a doctor since I had been pregnant. My mother was not in a good place to handle any of these things. She seemed to be very jealous, and very determined to make sure I knew that my father and Louise weren't saints, and they were no better than her. All I know, I was in a clean house with someone who cared about my wellbeing and the wellbeing of this baby. My mother didn't care how I felt at this point; our relationship was nonexistent. A few months before I had the baby, my father had a few legal troubles that required him to serve some time in jail. I didn't know for how long, but we had to move and I had to change schools. My mom saw this as an opportunity for us to mend our relationship. She found a place for us to move in, and this neighborhood was just as bad as the last, however, this time Louise was moving in with us. I knew if she was there things may not seem as bad. During this time, I enrolled in a new school, because I was in my last trimester, Louise and the guidance counselors advised me to attend a school for pregnant girls. The program was housed in a church directly across from the school. I was able to attend school there and catch the school bus home. After a month or two of getting settled in, I had met a young man named Wayne, would tell a few jokes, play in my hair, and strike up a conversation every chance he got. He was kinda cute and he lived in the neighborhood also. One day after getting off the bus, he was being his usual sarcastic funny self, joking and playing around, I turned my head, looked back to respond and when I turned back to the front, I ran smack dab into a big ass stop sign, that just happened to be the exact same height as me! Even though we were all laughing out of control, he came to check on me to make sure I was alright. After that day we were inseparable! All the while, I am trying to figure out why a boy would want to talk to me. I was six months pregnant, my stomach was all the way out there, and I was not feeling all that attractive, and most of all, IT WAS NOT HIS BABY! But he made me feel very special, and considering the state I was in, I definitely needed a friend! Yes, I knew he was a local dope boy who sold the very poison that my mom was using, and I knew my mom knew who he was to. We spent every day together; he was even there with Louise in the hospital when I had the baby. Louise even cut the umbilical cord! When I had to go back to school, Wayne's stepmom even helped out a few times with babysitting. While attending the pregnant school they would assist with different resources before and after the pregnancy. I had expressed that adoption would be a better option for me. I explained to my mom what I wanted to do but she was not supportive of the decision. How could I stay there with her and take care of a baby? By this time Louise had moved out of state, and some man who my mom met moved in, whom I found out later was a heroine user. I had to find an exit plan and quick. Over the course of a few months my mom would ask me, why do I want to give the baby up for adoption? For a moment in time she seemed to care about what was happening and going on with me. She came in my room sat down and began to tell me about something that happened to her when she was a young girl while she was dating. Several years ago, while out one night with some friends she was seeing a guy who she said she really liked and one night while she was visiting him, he attacked her sexually. I asked her, "Were you raped?" She expressed that she was very shaken up and scared by this situation and so ashamed, that she had not told a soul. My mom just looked at me, and I mean straight in the eye, and she asked me, "Were you raped, Tyishua?" I just broke down crying so hard, and it was at that very moment that I felt like that little girl who so desperately needed her mother the very night it took place. This would be the first time that I told anyone or said anything about how my first born was actually conceived. My auntie, who lived in California called me, and asked me if I had made a decision about the baby, I said no. She stated that she would take care of him and he would still be a part of the family, and he will know that you are his mom. She said, "I will be in town in a few weeks and we could discuss it then." I said, "This sounds good, but I still want to talk it over with my mom." It was close to the end of the summer and school was about to be back in session. I packed a bag to go stay at my grandmother's house so that the baby and I could spend some time with her. When my aunt arrived and we got together to go over to see my mom, we pulled up and I just saw people going in and out the front door like it was the corner store. We walked in and saw a group of about 6 to 8 people sitting in a circle just passing a crack pipe around! I was only gone for the weekend and the house had completely turned into a crack house. Even though my decision was an emotional one, I knew it would be best for my son and me. I honestly wanted to get on that plane with them, because I honestly had nowhere to go. My aunt talked with my grandmother and told her what had happened and that day, it was determined that I was going to stay with my Granny and Granddaddy! I now had some sense of normalcy. Even though this was the best and safest situation for me, I still had to hear it every now and again from my granny, what my mom and dad were not doing to help with taking care of me. After a few months, my mom lost her place, so she took a gig working as a live-in companion aid for an elderly woman who lived over an hour away from the city. That was short lived because it was too far from where she could get her supply. I knew she was going to be coming back soon. In the meanwhile, Wayne and I were still going strong. While living with his mom and aunt in another city, he picked up another hustle. Stealing cars! Wayne would never strike you as someone who would carry out any of the things that I am about to mention. Hell, I didn't think I would ever do any of the sort of things I'm about to mention. However, this was our means of survival. Selling drugs, robbing houses and sticking up dope boys were just to name a few. If you know anything about this life, then you know what comes with the territory. We truly were the modern-day Bonney and Clyde.

After moving from my grandmother's and back with my mom into another drug infested neighborhood, Wayne moved in shortly after his mom moved out of the state for a while with her sister. We both were able to attend the same high school, but I got pregnant with my second child while in my senior year of high school. Wayne dropped out to go full-time with the street life to set something up before our child was born. Things were spinning out of control. We had folks robbing us. Steal the cars that we stole, and breaking into our house to steal our money and drugs. Can we say, karma! And reality slapped me in my face after Wayne was involved in a 10 car high-speed police chase that led to me being arrested, not Wayne! How about them apples! An unmarked police car followed us after he noticed we were in a car that was reported stolen, that just happened to be a police officer's car! Of all the cars that we could have stolen,

I SUPPORT HER

what are the chances? Wayne told me to get out the car so that I could get away. I walked across the street to get on the bus and as I was taking a seat, I see Wayne getting on the bus and he sat behind me! I couldn't believe he got away, but I was so happy to see he was alright, until the cops pulled the bus over, I thought for sure he was going to jail forever, but they walked right past Wayne, and asked me to get off the bus! They didn't see his face during the chase, but remembered my big pregnant ass! As they took me in for questioning, they discovered I had a loaded .22 Dillinger in my purse. I didn't say a word about nothing, I was truly ride or die. I was arrested and charged that day for illegal possession of a gun. Scared, pregnant, and alone, I didn't know what to do, but I took one for the team. I prayed to God to please get me out of this, and my prayers were answered. The Commonwealth's Attorney wanted me to fess up to who was in the car, plus give up others, and also throw the book at me for having that gun. The Judge even said, "If I was walking the streets of that neighborhood, I would have a gun too." As the gavel went down, he announced, "Thirty days in jail, thirty days suspended, and a $100 fine!" THANK YOU, JESUS! After all of this, we found ourselves right back on the streets trying to find a place to live. After all of that, Wayne ended up getting in some trouble and getting locked up for a few months, leaving me to fend for myself. My mom was pillar to post, strung out and I had nowhere to stay. I stayed with who I could, where I could. I was 18, so I was able to register myself for school so that I could graduate. Yes, I was determined not to be a statistic! Nobody to wake me up, fix me breakfast, or encourage my day. I graduated from high school, but still living on the streets. I had my second baby, which was a high stress pregnancy, so I had a C-section. As I laid in the hospital each day, I was not sure where I was going to go. My mom said, "You can come live with me." I knew she was living in a crack house, but where was I going to go? I could not have my baby in this situation. Wayne's aunt said we could stay at her place, but for only 30 days. It was clean and safe. We were both able to find jobs, an apartment, and childcare within the 30 days! I also found resources that assisted with the first month's rent, deposit and electric bill deposit. I really wanted to go legit and do things on the up and up. I know it was nobody but God that got us this far. I finally was on the road to recovery. Shortly after moving in my Mother told me that she was diagnosed with the AIDS virus. I was devastated, but at this point, she lived her life even more carelessly and recklessly. She knew she was dying no matter what. She was fading away right before me day by day. She was found near death and ended up being hospitalized. During this time, Wayne and I had split. He still wanted to live that fast and loose life. So, I was back on the streets living here and there. My girlfriend, Mary, let me stay with her for a while. I looked for another place and our son went with Wayne's mom to Louisiana while I dealt with my mom's illness. My Aunt Pat couldn't stand to see her sister in this state, nor did she want her last days to be in hospice care, so she took her into her home and took care of her sister until her last breath. I fed my mother her last meal. This would be the last time I would ever hear her say my name, laugh, cry, yell, or pray with me. The woman that laid before me was not the woman I knew as the beautiful, vibrant, mother, sister, aunt, and friend to so many. I wanted to remember her the way she was, before all of this. My mother was 44 years old when her sun set February 3rd, 1995. Honestly, I never had a chance to grieve my mother's death. Too busy getting my life in order.

I was still sleeping on someone's couch when my mom died. However, I did meet someone during this time who would later shift my life in a completely different direction. You thought this was something? Honey, wait until you read *Who Said I was Done?*!

During the course of everything I endured, I didn't know what path my life was taking. Sometimes I didn't have time to think or even ask myself the question, "Which way should I go?" I just jumped in, head first! Taking whatever route looked the shortest or easiest. Through the unknown, I had no choice but to trust God. My bumps and bruises could have been way more severe. I could have done like so many others that went through the same or similar experiences and turned to drugs, had a host of unwanted pregnancies, abortions, committed suicide, sexually abused others, continued a life of crime – or worse, being killed. Dealing with countless episodes of bullying, sexual assaults, and depression, you ask, how did I allow myself to still love and trust people, in spite of? How was I being able to enjoy relationships and marriage? Why didn't I just give up? The answer to that question is, at the turn of every situation, there was something, or someone there to help me. Remembering who God was and is, who I was, and where I came from. Even with all the dysfunction, I thank God for a strong and firm family foundation. As my Aunt Vivian used to say, "We come from 'good stock' and we are cut from a different cloth!" God allowed me to go through, endure, and live to tell the story that has shaped me into the very woman I am today. There was and is someone who was told not to tell theirs, or there may be someone who still hasn't forgiven themselves or others for going through and experiencing some of these situations or worse. I brought you all into my world because you can stand firm and give your testimony without shame or persecution. Live your life courageously, because you are not defeated, you are strength! After crawling, walking and running through all I went through, I knew there was something tremendous, bold, beautiful, bright and full of color awaiting me. I just had to have enough faith and patience, a heart that believed, a mind that was willing, and the courage to take action. I leave this with you this:

Isaiah 61:3 To console those who mourn in Zion, to give them beauty for ashes, the oil of joy for mourning, the garment of praise for the spirit of heaviness, the planting of the Lord, that He may be glorified.

On the other side of your pain, you will find your purpose.

CHAPTER 9

For My Good but For His Glory

"Coming Up The Rough Side Of The Mountain"

By: Tabisha AnnQuaneete McCoy

I remember it like it was yesterday. The dusk had come; I was standing in front of the refrigerator. Darkness filled the room. My life changed forever. I had to carry a burden; this thing I called a curse. I remember like it yesterday. In 1984 at age nine, I was diagnosed with Tourette's syndrome (TS). TS is characterized as a multiple schema of complex, simple, vocal, and physical tics. TS wasn't easy to have; it was rare at the time and many medical professionals were just embarking on the existence of this disorder. TS was hard to diagnose and treat. Being rare the only medicine used to treat TS was Haldol at the time. I'd rather have the frequency of the tics than take Haldol. Haldol caused extreme weight gain, swelling of the joints and even caused me to feel sedated. TS was so perplexed and even distorted to say the least. Even during my initial evaluation, my neurologist said, "Oh boy, she has Tourette's". My heart dropped in my legs and I jumped. This time it wasn't Tourette's. I didn't know about Tourette's, but I just knew my life would change forever.

Once I returned from the doctors with my final diagnosis, I laid on my bed; and I thought what about my friends? Imagine that, my friends were my first thought. Honestly, I didn't think of my mom first because I knew my mom to be a superwoman. My mom was a strong, unmovable, and unshakeable. I had never witnessed a storm in my mom's life where the storm moved her out of position. The saying the closet person to a mother is her child is very true. Little did I know, I would often hear my mom crying in her room or coming out her room with red eyes? Unspoken words, how is my child going to make it in this world? Or the world doesn't care anything about her, what did I do wrong? To prove to my mom that I was going to be alright; I acted well. I was going to beat this; this THING, mimicking someone who declared war on cancer. My mom may have been my second thought, but right then she was the only one I was willing to fight for or with. However, I realized quickly, fighting behind closed doors was the easy part, but wait I must go out from these four walls into a place called world. The very thing that frightened mom. After weeks of re-cooperating and my mom's war room talks; we decided I would go back to school. During this time, I attended Buggs Elementary with long hallways, shining floors, and the sound of raging waters (children). I found that children can be so blunt, without tact, not even thinking on how words can stick forever. Not only, were the children mean, but very torrent. I, on the other hand; was coming back to a world I wasn't ready for. I thought to myself just control yourself, breathe and move slowly. During the day, I was calmer than expected with a little noticeable tic that I could pass off as something else. I thought to myself "this may be easier than I thought". I mastered that day, but I had more days to go. If I had to say, what were my most challenging years of my life? I would say grades 4th through 8th grade, educating teachers about a behavior that seemed to be a behavior of a class clown was very difficult. Class clowns were known or vocal outbursts, eye twitching, and flickering of the tongue. These tics were just a few I had in the first phase of Tourette's. Explaining to teachers that I shouldn't go to in-school suspension was extremely stressful for me because it forced me to hold the tics back, which made the intensity and frequency increase. Holding back a tic is like a balloon having too much air, and it pops. I popped a lot!

My mom and I thought having a meeting with the administrators would be beneficial for me; at least we would be on the same page. The meeting went well; until the administrators wanted to put me in special education. My mom, my superwoman was ready to take the whole school board down. I remember the whole board was quiet, as my Grandmother Dora would say," You could hear a pin drop". You see my mom fought because she knew that learning to overcome starts early, if I had been placed in a special education class, I would have stayed in a special education class. My mom didn't want me going down, she wanted my teachers to come up. It's not the beginning of a place that matters but it's the ending, it is how you finish. When I told my grandmother Dora about the meeting she said" I would have like to be a fly on the wall". My grandmother Dora and all the sayings she had. I smile often about the words she'd say, those sayings have kept me, and guided me on this journey. Sayings such as "What don't kill you, will only make you stronger," "You don't live this life for nobody; because when you die, you go alone; so live your life and live it well," or "When a person shows you who they are, believe them."

I returned to school from the meeting, not having to be in a special education class. My mom was hard on me, because the world and my teachers would be harder. I would study at the kitchen table, tic and all. I don't make light of my tics by far, I just learned to laugh; because I cried so many nights, "Lord, take this thing from me." My neurologist told us I was depressed because I was withdrawn, but I was depressed because the kids at school picked on me and called me names such as jumping bean. The pressure of not being who I was, and who I have now overwhelmed me and caused me to exclude myself. Truthfully, my peers already had done that anyway. I struggled in many areas, but I really struggled with me. I often refer to Romans 7: 15 & 17 *I do not understand my own actions, I do not practice what I wish, but I do the very thing that I Loathe. However, it is no longer I who do the deed; but the sin which has possession of me.*

Honestly, I have this thorn because God allowed it, and it keeps me humble. Not saying it was meant for me to have this disorder but I will say God allowed it to take course in my life. Eventually, all things come to an expected end, and I believe God is a God of productivity – He can produce out of any situation. *Therefore, being justified by faith, we have peace with God through our Lord Jesus Christ. By whom also we have access by faith into His grace wherein we stand, rejoice in hope of the Glory of God. And we not only so but we Glory in tribulations also: knowing that tribulation worked patience; and patience, experience; and experience, hope* (Romans 5: 1-4 KJV).

One thing I know is that I have been conditioned for this journey. I have been built for this road. I believe God can make me great having

Tourette's. I also believe that on this journey I will have what and who I need. His grace is enough for me. The world fails to see that we all have mountains in our lives; we tend to minimize everyone's journey. My mountain may not be your mountain, my valley low may not be your valley low; but the truth of the matter is, regardless of whose valley or mountain it is, we have to take it and walk it out until the end.

Tourette's has been extremely difficult for me, the decisions and choices I had to make have been rough; but I did it. Not just for me, but for others who are on the rough side of the mountain and see my mountain. As I become more spiritually mature, I realized that this thing I identified as a curse, has been a steppingstone for me. It has catapulted me to a place where I can thrive and make myself better. I have seen a lot; I have heard so many things and experienced a lot; but I am grateful because I have a foundation that has been built that man nor Tourette's can shake. You see, I have Tourette's, but Tourette's don't have me. We don't always experience trials for ourselves; sometimes we go through for the sake of others. God in saw this even in my mother's womb before the foundations of the world. What I learned was Romans 8:28, how even TS was working to fashion and mold me to be who I am today, I learned that it is working for my good, but for his glory. All the tears I cried, all the lonely times I had were moments for God to work in me and to build me up, and to have me quiet so He could show me just what I am meant to be. Don't think people didn't try to tell me who I was or size me up. That's what people do when they want to keep you in a box or see that you are gifted by infected. See, I was useful to so many, but when I wanted to get my wings clipped TS became such an obstacle, so they say. Again, sizing up my journey; trying to tell me who God is to me.

When you are on your way up a rough mountain and you hear a lot of noise, know that the noise you hear is a direct indicator that your "thing" will work for your good. God's ways are perfect and there are no mistakes His doings. He knew this book was coming forth and he knew that I would address your mountain. *For I know the thoughts I think toward you, saith the Lord, thoughts of peace, and not of evil, to give; an expected end* (Jeremiah 29:11 KJV. Know the journey may get rough and the mountain may seem high; but you will get through it. Walk it out because in your process, God is doing something wonderful and greater in you. *Yea, though I walk through the valley of the shadow of death, I will fear no evil: for thou art with me; thy rod (grace) and thy staff (mercy) they comfort me* (Psalms 23:4 KJV).

We all have that rough time and the rough side; but it's for our making and ultimate purpose. Again, I say I have Tourette's, but Tourette's don't have me. If I talked in depth about TS and the dynamics of TS, you would have identified me as Tourette's, but I talked about me having the advantage.

TS is a type of Tic Disorder. The tics are involuntary, repetitive movements and vocalizations. The onset of Tourette's is usually in childhood with neurodevelopmental conditions. What's the difference between tics and Tourette syndrome? The movements and vocalizations are called tics. A formal diagnosis of Tourette syndrome is met when at least one year has passed since the onset of the first tic, and the patient has experienced at least one phonic tic and at least two motor tics. TS is often accompanied by other conditions, such as attention deficit hyperactivity disorder (ADHD) and obsessive-compulsive disorder (OCD). The disorder is named after Dr. Georges Gilles de la Tourette, the pioneering French neurologist who in 1885 first described the condition in an 86-year-old French noblewoman. The error people make is categorizing TS as a mental illness, it is not. TS is a neurological disorder where the chemicals in the brain that transmit nerve impulses (neurotransmitters), such as dopamine and serotonin backfires. Although the exact incidence of Tourette syndrome is uncertain, it is estimated to affect 1 to 10 in 1,000 children. This disorder occurs in populations and ethnic groups worldwide, and it is more common in males than in females. TS is a very peculiar disorder, that often leave people puzzled its unusual, uncommon symptoms. It takes a strong person to deal with TS because of the burden we carry in our bodies based on the intensity of the tics. It's a complex disorder likely caused by a combination of inherited (genetic) and environmental factors.

I mentioned to you earlier in the chapter about the simple and complex tics, now I will take you a little further with the type of tics you may see. Simplex tics: consists of eye blinking, jerking of the limbs, shrugging of shoulders and facial grimacing. Complex tics: consists of muscle tics in groups that are purposeful in appearance such as jumping, hopping and twirling. You also have a very misunderstood symptom of Coprolalia, involuntary outburst of obscene words or socially inappropriate and derogatory remarks. Although Coprolalia is the most widely known symptom of TS, it occurs in only a small number of patients with TS. Talk about guarding your ear gates and eye gates, this was very challenging for me and sometimes still is. Symptoms can come and go as well as change quite frequently. Symptoms often progress into more complex tics as the child reaches adolescence. This is believed to be caused by puberty/hormones. An individual will not fully 'outgrow' their tics; however, symptoms often decrease as a person age. However, for those with severe forms of the disorder and with severe comorbidities, TS may interfere with the individual's everyday life and activities of school, home, or work, such as being educated to their full potential, obtaining a job/career, gaining independence, and having meaningful relationships with family. Tourette's is such a rare, hard to treat disorder and often depict as demonization or witchcraft; but sparks curiosity of how one lives and adjusts with the frequency and intensity of tics over a span of time.

CHAPTER 10

Return to Sobriety

"Surviving to Thriving"

By: Toni Ferguson

My disease – "Dis-ease" was my greatest teacher and healer.

Here I sit today in eagerness for the day. But it wasn't always like that. I choose to start my story at what I call the point of my rock bottom. This is the point that brought me to today, which is a success in the making. It starts in the middle of a divorce when the Guardian ad litem took my two girls. I survived a divorce that took about 3 years and 3 attorneys. I allowed it to drag me to the bowels of hell. That was just the beginning of my low point.

I was so deep into an addiction of alcohol and Xanax; I could not get my brain free to function. My rock bottom was its own dark path within my life journey.

I SUPPORT HER

The good news is that I am not alone. Instead of unconditional love and proper intervention, there are members of society that will decide who the "weak" members of the family and take steps to kick them out of the family "nest". Why? In this case, ego, greed, hate, jealousy, and inheritance. I had two elderly parents that were over medicated and caught in their own addiction of old way thinking. I had and still have a sister that has hated me since I was born. I had a husband that had had enough of my drinking and wanted to be free. Understand that I am not judging them, but I am identifying them for their behaviors. I also want to state that my experience with outside help – counseling was a huge detriment to society at large. In my opinion, all the doctors/ counselors wanted to do was to diagnose me and my AA friends a disease. They wanted to label us with a mental health illness and drug the hell out of us!!! In my case I was dead on.

I will start with my sister. Mom has told the story for many years that I was born when she was 10 years old. During a night of teething and crying, my sister rushed into their bedroom and told my parents not to ever pull a dirty trick on them like that again. Mom and Dad had been married for 17 years when I entered the world… so I was a surprise. My sister was a red headed girl with mental issues treated by a psychiatrist. She cut the upper pads of her fingers at a very young age because Daddy called her a "sissy". Daddy was a WWII Army Sergeant, no girls in his family and a child of survivors of the Depression of the 1920's. The war taught him to kill or be killed. That kind of life did not teach him how to address a little daughter. She had an abusive teacher in early first years of school that Mom and Dad did not properly handle. She even pulled out her eye lashes…Such behavior appears to be textbook then due to the abuse of some teachers. I did not have any of that. I was, blonde and happy and endless energy. I was a major thorn in her side. All I wanted was to be loved and a part of my sister's life. She had other plans from day one!

As our adult years have taken place, she was married five times, DUI, and a long list of debts. Nothing is ever her fault and she has always had what she thinks is a sound diagnosis or defined conclusion of everyone else's problems… or are they really problems? Are they just what she has judged as a "problem"? She sells herself as a great expert in general.

My ex-husband comes from two parents in a small town with the height of dysfunctional behaviors. He had an interesting life of abuses from very ignorant and abusive dad and mom that lived in fear and denial. People knew his dad in that town; how he was and what he did but did nothing about his actions in work or private. But I saw my ex as sweet and full of love and wanted to break free and have a good life.

He developed great talent in sports and a good student, but he saw himself as a victim and was afraid of his parents and what they would think or do. Through our first years of being together I discovered his problems and fears. I connected with counseling and put him on a path of self - discovery healing and love. I showed him how to cook, improve gardening skills, people skills, and I got him out of that sick parental entanglement and into a new location and freedom. He totally blossomed and became a good, strong, loving man. When our children were tiny, he was the best daddy!! I loved so many things about him. He had my heart and soul. We were together over 20 years. I will always have a love for him and our journey. I hope he will a fare well through the outcoming of the truth and the exposure of the actions he has taken in malice and vein to keep me away from our children. I am now clean and sober for over 5 years Notwithstanding we have had no contact in five years I believe he knows

I am clean and sober. My mom made it clear to my sister and to him. It is as if he is hiding behind my sister and her lies. Reviewing my phone recordings of my mom and her e-mails, it no longer matters. When the truth surfaces both will face consequences on many levels.

To give a little more detail over 20+ years of life with him, I handled his parents, I got him out of a small town and into a larger city and into the development of a good solid career. He became more of his own person. He was so devoted to me and I adored him. We created two beautiful girls that are four years apart. Together we began to grow and break free of old thinking of what we were supposed to do and be. We were both children of alcoholics…functioning alcoholics. These parents were somehow able to keep a job and build a foundation. But there were endless moments of hell dealing with these two sets of parents. I believe we both allowed them to drive us apart.

Now a bit about me. I started drinking when I was about 12. I was out fishing with my dad and we ran out of soda. This was the time before bottled water. I was told not to tell my mother. Half of my childhood was in the Outer Banks of NC, and for the most part it was magical!! At least that is what I thought. The other part was in a City in Virginia that barely came out of a farming community. To me was a sickening version of good 'ole boy society. My mom performed the necessary daily housewife duties. The house was clean, the food was delicious, there were trips and outings to many nice things and places. I did not recognize she was drunk almost every night. She lived her life in worry over one thing after another. Life in general seemed to scare her. My dad worked many hours, and then would come home and work in the back yard huge garden. My parents were good to me and I am grateful for a wonderful overall childhood.

I SUPPORT HER

Drinking and parties were a way of life. No one thought of it as a bad thing or something that would cause hardships. As I got older, I was going to private clubs and social occasions with my parents and drinking a little by little. It was the thing to do. I was seldom around children of my age as my parents were so much older and had already lived that life. I was so geared to adult conversation and issues, I blended right in! It was remarked so many times that I was such an "adult". Mom would say I was born 40. I did not know back then I was learning to use this substance to escape the things that were uncomfortable in life. I drank through college, and after. I married a college sweetheart, (first husband) who was a child of phenomenally successful parents and total pros at drinking. They were wealthy upstanding citizens of a small town. They were very well connected. We traveled and experienced a life among the wealthy and highly educated. That bling went to dirt quick. I saw and experienced mental and physical, abuse and anger and ignorance, and I got out. My first husband drank more than I did. He had a successful career and power. As time passed, (ten years total) he became a nasty bully. He informed me it was his right to expect me to bear his children. He labeled me as stupid unattractive and not particularly important. I was tormented but I broke free. I married my second husband not afraid of anything!! I was convinced that I could accomplish anything, and I could handle any bully I needed to handle. The second set of in-laws were the spitting image of the Flintstones!! I broke the fear they engrained into the mind of my second husband and guided him away from a tunnel of past abuse. I put them in their place several times. It was total shock and awe. That is what I thought. I was partly right. I knew it all and I was still drinking.

At forty, I hit a huge depression. I had just had my second child and I was so upset at getting older. I was very unhappy as we had a good life, but it was not good enough. We were programed to concentrate on lack. Hence our uphill climb was tough and did not need to be. We grew apart. We moved into a larger house. It was a fantastic neighborhood and his job was good and sound. I maintained admin type work. We had money coming in. The family dream was coming together but I was falling apart. I was closet drinking every night. I began hiding bottles. I randomly went to 5 or 6 different stores to buy my cheap chardonnay and beer. I hid the alcohol everywhere. My ex went on a second conference with his job with one of his female co-workers and I knew they had something. I did not know exactly the extent their relationship, but I could feel the bond was beyond friendship. She was my friend, his subordinate, her husband was a friendly heavy drinker and our daughters were friends. Their commonality was drinking spouses. To this day I wonder if she realizes she was a home wrecker... or at least corporative component. I had my first breakdown and attended a week outpatient program to deal with drinking. During trying to get sober, played the red solo cup video for me. This was a video on YouTube that showed common base people drunk out of their mind singing laying around in pools and in little clothing. He was a fan of Family Guy. I hated it. He gave me a Christmas gift of the main character of The Family Guy naked holding a gift box in front of him. He thought that was funny and posted it on his Facebook. I still have that and the FB page. It was after my first attempt to get sober that he created a Facebook page. He started running to get in shape. I thought that was wonderful. But I did not know he was doing this as if he was a single man. He portrayed himself as single. He kept that page a secret. To this day I know very little about what I call "Nosebook". My sister was really into it. She somehow discovered his page and exposed him. She at that time was on my side, (at least she had me thinking that). She even luckily caught my ex and his little running buddy at lunch together at a Quizno's sitting together in our Town and Country Van talking. That pretty co-worker (ten years my junior) became his running buddy – or that was his claim. The pictures of him with his arms around her and their intense connection sent me back to the bottle!! I was worse than ever. I was enraged and hurt. Finally, he was over the marriage. He was gathering what he considered evidence I was an unfit wife and parent. He took pictures of my bottles and of my Xanax bottles. My sister discovered this too and told me about it. She wanted me to get straight and get back on track. I rushed to get an attorney as I was done with his disloyalty and sneakiness. He ignored me over the years and did very little to help with the children as they got older. The teachers and principals did not like him. A few told me he was a jerk. Funny… so did my third attorney. He had a habit of sitting and staring at the boob tube and would never hear me or the kids. I knew this is not who he really was. He was acting out of a result of his own emotions. I could not completely judge him. I still loved him!! My answer was to drink.

It took a what seemed forever for us to short sell the house and to physically separate into different dwellings. We lived together in the same house for some time as a "separated couple". While working my mom found a house. She financially helped me get this little home for me and the girls and to get away from this "Jive Turkey", as my ex-husband began to close out our banking accounts and then tell me about it after the fact. My girls told me what he was doing. They thought he was a jerk. I loved him. He had my heart and soul. I could not say anything against him. I was too shocked and hurt. We made children together. I was a drinker – an alcoholic! I saw myself as the bad person and was angry and deeply hurt at my own behavior and the fact I could not stop. I wanted help so bad. Back then no one around me had any clue what to do. And those who did were not in favor of my success. During the separation in two different dwellings, the girls were ordered by the courts to go back and forth week on week off. The courts really make children suffer!! This process must change. My youngest constantly came back to me with cuts, burn blisters or some kind wound as she was barely watched. My oldest daughter became the second mommy. My mom bought me a car and kept it in their names until the divorce so that he could not claim the car. They paid for counseling for both girls so they could get through the divorce ok. They told the counselor they wanted to be with me and were not happy with their dad's behavior. I still have all of this documentation and I eventually will use it.

When my sister found out all that my parents were doing to help me, she became beyond enraged.

During the divorce I went through 2 horrible attorneys!! They drug out the process and sucked out way too much money. Finally, by the time I had the third attorney and he saved me!! By that long drawn out time of misery and fear and no sleep... I was beyond help!! My drinking was out of control. I was so hungry for love and affection. I met a former Special Ops Marine that told me he loved me. He really did. He was getting clean and sober at the time. He was almost divorced as well. He had been sober and married with 2 kids for 20 years. However, he relapsed and lost his police career of just before 20 years. But he loved ME and I was so hungry for love and affection and so hurt and angry at the little pretty running buddy I started a relationship with a man who became a manipulative gas lighter from hell!!! Through all the mess I do not regret that 5 years on and off, of that relationship. I became strong. I learned who I was and what I wanted in life. His behavior helped me to identify my sister's actions. I learned what narcissism and gaslighting was. I learned the true meaning of defamation of character.

My sister conspired with my mom to have me committed to a psych institution. She wrote about obsessions and my behavior descriptions on the Emergency Custody Order that were not true and got Mom to sign it.

As I spent a few days in that place, she was trying to make them keep me longer. The did not work as the judge who knew Dad dismissed me. He knew I was not crazy, but that I needed to stop drinking. The doctors who work in these institutions do not care if you get sober. They task themselves with choosing some mental illness diagnosis and start pumping mind altering drugs into your body. Lovely professionals!!! While I was tucked away my sister broke into my house and stole well over 2500.00 of my personal property. My name was the ONLY name on my lease and she had absolutely no substantial permission whatsoever to invade my private home. Outside of my house were over 90 Walmart storage boxes of personal property. She opened all of them went through the items inside each one. She and my ex-husband helped themselves to what they wanted and left the tops of the boxes off. So almost everything was ruined. When I returned it snowed and the wreckage of my belongings were frozen along with trash strewn all over the back yard. I have pictures that will identify the hands of my sister and ex-husband. I got out saw this and tried to get back into a normal life. But I was still without my children and I was caught in a miserable toxic cycle of my sister and mom. I was committed again within a few months. But this time she managed to get the keys from the property management and get into my house again. She disheveled my house even worse than when I left it and took over 100 pictures. She sent them to my mom. She would mix them with pictures and make media like contrived comments like what a drunk mom cannot do so the dad has to do everything. She opened personal mail from my attorney and other documents and took pictures of them. She stole my 2 cats. She gave one away to a friend of her son's and put one in a shelter. She told my mom that I was never going back to my house but would have to be in a city program for the mentally disabled.

I have e-mails from Mom telling about my sister behind the scenes of second ECO. She was back in the Emergency room talking from doctor to nurse and others about me. She was getting information from the staff, blow by blow and emailing the details to Mom. She was pumping with emergency staff with lies of how crazy I was!! She could not wait for me to be carried away back to the psych hospital!! I was drunk out of my mind. That does not mean I was crazy. But everyone bought her story. During my second stay, my assigned doctor assigned mind altering drugs and diagnosed me with schizoreactive disorder. Mind you, I was not free and clear of my alcohol. That takes way more than 10 days to clear. No one has any right to diagnose a person that is not free and clear of all medications. Oh, but they do!!! This doctor was successful to pump me with drugs there. I am not yet done with that doctor. I will further write the Board of Health with my story. Since then, every medical professional I have spoken with has said nothing good about this guy. Yet he has followed such damaging procedures with other innocent people that just needed to get sober.

Moving forward my sobriety date is April 24, 2015. I was kept in that horrible establishment for 10 days where I was wrongly diagnosed and fed a few mind-altering drugs.

But after ten days I came back. I tossed out all the wine bottles. I was free of the benzos and took the *crap* mind altering meds this whack job prescribed and put them in a case. I still have them today to remind me of how cruel and abusive some members of the medical society can be and how far I have come. I had to start healing from these horrible hardships and press forward.

I stayed with my folks for my first week, got back one of my cats, and got temp job assignments within less than a month. I started back with AA and was determined to reach a successful first year of sobriety. I rocked it!!!

During the first few years I was getting sober, one of my part time jobs was working on a farm that has a petting zoo and pony rides. During my working hours my sister showed up and snuck around taking pictures of me. She took pictures of the whereabouts of my car and report to Mom I was not working but staying at home drinking. I had my marine boyfriend drive me to work and keep my car in my driveway so she would not know where I was working. I have emails and phone calls recorded where my sister told Mom that I was not really working when I was. I started recording phone calls as I knew one day, I would have a case. I knew one day I would prove my sanity, sobriety, and my successes!! But I had to start documentation every which way I could. I feared for my mom's safety as I put nothing past my sister's motives. Mom would call me and ask where I was. Finally, I had my boyfriend call Mom and set that record straight. Mom told me that my sister swore it was too cold for the farm to operate and was not open when in fact it was. When my mom would tell her about me receiving my chips for 3, 6, 9 and 12 months of sobriety from Alcoholics Anonymous, she would tell mom that it was a lie and I could get those chips anywhere. At the same time, she would contact me, and act like the loving sister. She would tell me how hateful mom was and about all of the ailments she had. I still have text after text from my loving sister slandering Mom. One day while my sister was at Mom's house, Mom took a nap, my sister took a picture of her sleeping. Upon awaking she informed Mom she had COPD. My mom's doctor of course dismissed that radical idea. As I took on full time jobs, I would not tell Mom where I was working so she would not let my sister know. The other people working on that farm told them how my sister would reach out to their friends to tell them how crazy I was. What kind of a sister does such things?? On one particular recorded phone call, my mom tells me she had to straighten out my oldest daughter. She informed Mom she knew I was still drinking and that I stole pillows and other items out of my mom's house. At this point I was more than a year sober. Mom was so sad that my ex and sister were still determined to pump these lies into the heads of my daughters. I cannot count the days and nights of hardship!! My sister continued working hard to convince my parents I was not only a drunk but I was also crazy…mentally ill!!! I have emails from my mom reporting my sister at her house digging on her computer for ideas from Google to define my mental state and diagnose me. She did a great job!!

I climbed from temporary assignment to assignment to a full-time job. I left that one to take care of elderly parents. My mom's doctor had her on Ativan; up to 3 mg of it per day. He went for ten months without checking her. Her issues were never properly dealt with. She ended up in a hospital and diagnosed after several days, (her doctor is horrible!!), with spinal stenosis and went into a short-term rehab. I got into the shipyard world just before the big layoffs and got a great start with even more valuable skills. During that time, Mom got out of rehab from spinal stenosis, and my sister took over the care of her and Dad. My sister threw out the PT and OT assigned to Mom. My mom wanted them back and she would not abide with my Mom's wishes. Within a month or so Mom was back in the hospital and with other health factors. By that time, I was completely free of the Marine and even though I was laid off I managed to hold 1 to 3 jobs at a time. So much for Schizoreactive Disorder!!!

I finally landed a job I loved!! And I broke free of my marine boyfriend. But I no longer had time to take care of Mom and Dad. They by that time told me that my sister was not working full time and came in good. She seldom maintained a full-time job. She had an issue showing up on time and she always know how the owners could run their companies. They knew it was time for me to really get on my feet. I was excited and ready!!

I temped From January to April at this shipyard. During that time, I received two letters of recommendation and good friendships/acquaintances. I worked a "home shop" position at a grocery store and again at the same farm. I also held more temp office/admin positions as well. Any visits my girls had with my parents had to be when I was not there and under my sister's observation along with my ex. I have an email from Mom telling of a visit where my oldest daughter had to whisper to my mom, she loved me. She told my dad during that visit too. I have precious pictures included in that particular email. I have since shared that email with several people and may publish it.

My last phone call with my mom was not a great one. My sister and my mom's nurse recounted to her my conversation with the nurse. So, Mom told me she did not want to see me. I embarrassed her by telling her nurse what my sister had done by throwing out her PT and OT and I planned to sue her one day. Mom was always against any dirty laundry discussed with outside members of the family. Our elephant in the room was not one but a herd of elephants!! My mom told me she agreed with my sister that I was crazy and did not want to see me.

Shortly thereafter my mom passed. I was temping at a shipyard subcontractor in purchasing when Mom passed. Before I was laid off from the first shipyard position, my mom went back to the hospital and on to another rehab... such great care from my sister... who knows. At that point I had to start letting go of the toxic and keep pushing forward. I tried to get help from a few attorneys with my mom and even called adult protective services. They all sucked!!!

My sister had her high school friend (they graduated from high school in 1974) call me to tell me. She told me there would be no ceremony or memorial and she would be cremated. Half of that was a big stinking lie! That was a total lie as I spoke with a cousin at the grocery store. She told me her dad attended my mom's memorial. My sister did not want me included. It was all a successful plan of hers to drive me out of the family. It is ok as they could not separate me from my mom even in her transition. There is no such thing as death. I knew this but I was still so hurt and devastated. Somehow, I knew I had to keep on moving forward. I could feel without a doubt my mom was at peace and was ok. But how my sister handled it was turpitude!! That was three years ago. I still grieve. I still hurt sometimes. But Mom is with me.

In those three years, I have been dating a wonderful man with a good management position and we share a great, healthy, fun life. I have a cat, bunny and budgies that I love. I have been blessed with a roommate that has become like an aunt, a life coach, and spiritual teacher all in one. My roommate and I have gone totally organic. I am successfully practicing organic gardening. Along with my roommate, I have an organic based blog, a hydroponic tower in the kitchen full of delicious greens, and a plan for a woman owned organic business that is now in its first steps. I am an upper level Admin to two very accomplished Directors in a privately owned shipyard. I have had two promotions and two certificates of impact within less than two years of permanent employment. I have rediscovered myself. I got through a bankruptcy, bought a car and my credit score is up to the ability to buy my first house with my roommate. I take no meds. I am even off my thyroid meds and feel better than ever. I do this with proper research, herbs, clean diet, and meditation. And absolutely no doctors!!! I may try a holistic doctor eventually, but I will always recheck the info they give. My general practicing doctors failed me. I do not blame them as many of them have become like zombies of the old ways and beliefs. The good news it there is hope for them too. We are evolving as a species as we have arrived at an age of The Awakening. Evil is bubbling up and our collective love and gradual awareness is growing and healing our world!!

How did I do this? My roommate and I together discovered the same life experiences and how to heal from them. We both went through a divorce, had dysfunctional parents and siblings. And we both have listened studied and practiced gratitude, meditation and a whole new way of thinking and living.

I constantly read in depth about Epigenetics, Neuroendocrinology, Heart /Brain Coherence. I read and listen to everything I can from: Dr. Joe Dispenza, Gregg Braden, Anthony Williams the Medican Medium, Dr. Christiane Northrup, and the like.

Through all of this I still have days of pain, anguish, and anger that I still do not yet have my girls and they do not know I am thriving. I still cannot afford an attorney. My final divorce papers dictate that I must have a psych eval to prove I am capable of parenting. Back when my mom was alive, I started my eval. It cost $2500.00. I paid all but $900.00. From the first rehab, my mom of sound mind, wrote me a check to cover that last $900.00 and help with the rent. My sister used my dad to intercept that check. I am now seeking to complete that eval to go to court. I have also learned that the actions against me performed by my sister and my ex who has hidden behind her, involve parental alienation. Telling my two girls that I am still drinking, a thief, a liar, etc. is not legal.

I am very competent with children!!! I even kept the daughter of my ex-boyfriend for many weekends before and after we broke up. Her mom and I are friends and to this day we are very close. I got her involved in horseback riding. During 2016 I became a 4H volunteer. I have not been able to attend with my new career as much as I'd like, but I love this!! My dear friend is a 4H director in the equine division. I became close friends with a single parent and her daughter. This young girl just happened to be in class with Hailey. She finally told my oldest daughter about me. This student also showed me how to create an Instagram account. I was able to follow and make connection with equestrian students all around the world and still do today. My oldest daughter connected with me through her Instagram she was able to post a picture of her and my youngest. I knew this post was specifically for me. Upon her dad discovering the connection he threw a huge fit and called my sister. She went nuts and yelled at my parents telling them I was a liar and a drunk. I do not know all of the specifics, but I do have recorded phone calls and emails to use once I could afford to expose this horrible treatment. Neither my ex nor my sister had any right to make my daughter dissolve her social media accounts or be angry with them or to feed them any negative false information.

I will have my record set straight with my entire family and expose what was done.

Now soon I will have that eval, an attorney, and numerous friends and colleagues called to action to confirm my deeds of sanity, and goodness. My record will finally be set straight. Nothing will stop me.

I have learned that out of the 70-80,000 thoughts I have daily, I had to change them. I had to go beyond my comfort zone and learn how to love, forgive and heal. I have learned that knowledge is power and that self-knowledge is self-power. I know I am by no means alone in my journey. I know we are all connected. And I know the truth comes out no matter how pretty my sister paints that canvas to her convenience. Evil bubbles up, the truth cleans and sets life straight and thriving again. My children will see me soon. They will know a better me. They will see the actual facts and see my healing. They will see I've gone from ground zero to full throttle thriving.

I do still have my mom. Energy can neither be created or destroyed. She is still with me but as a healed energy of light and love. My dad is now 93. Due to all of the toxic deed of my sister I have not seen him. I miss and would like very much to see him. But he must be told by a professional person of my sanity to wipe clean the layers of her lies. If I do not see him before he makes a transition, I will still have his love and energy with me and it will be of true enlightenment and understanding of how things have really been. I no longer live in the old beliefs as I know now a belief is just a thought you keep on thinking. It is seldom fact. I know we are all energy.

I feel the energy of my girls and they feel mine. We will physically connect again soon. No matter the evil and lies, the love between a child and parent can never be destroyed. With the truth being exposed it will grow stronger no matter the pain and anger the love is still there. I know what I think about I bring about. I am blessed with numerous like-minded people pulling for me and believing in me. They know my love, commitment, loyalty, ever developing abilities, and the person I am becoming. The past will take a back seat to the light of today. I believe it will help those who have been in the same web of darkness. I can now thank my mom and dad for all of the good and bad. Now I can thank my ex-husband and not judge him. The courts and karma will take care of that as I continue to thrive. I own my alcoholism and past actions. I have paid my price and I have healed. I have made peace with myself and function quite well. I am not co-dependent and I do not practice enablement. I, however, do not deserve the lies and defamation created against me. My mother called this cruel and unusual punishment and it is.

ABOUT THE AUTHORS

Danielle Ferreira

C.E.O, Caged Bird Publishing

Business Consultant, Literary Manager & Graphic Designer, Author, Veteran, PTSD & Mental Health Advocate. Earned a M.A Business Management with an Undergrad in Electrical Mechanical Technology.

www.cagedbirdpublishing.com

FB cagedbirdpublishingllc

Instagram cagedbirdpublishingllc

Albertina Dancy

C.E.O, Great Pathway Counseling Services LLC, Gospel Recording Artist, Evangelist speaker & Mental Health Advocate. Earned a M.A in Human Services Counseling, B.A in Criminal Justice and current working on her Doctorate in Forensic Psychology

FB https://www.facebook.com/albertinadancy1

Instagram iamalbertinadancy

www.greatpathwayCS.com

I SUPPORT HER

Gloria Eason

30 yrs. Shipbuilding & Repair, Steel Metal Supervisor
BA in Business w/minor in Engineering

FB https://www.facebook.com/gloria.j.eason

Tiffanie Shelton

CEO Teal Box Cosmetics, Licensed Practical Nurse, Cervical Cancer Outreach Advocate.

FB: https://www.facebook.com/TifTif27

www.tealboxcosmetics.com

Tyishua McCoy-Brown

Founder, Director & CEO at Build Not Break, Singer Songwriter, Colour U Cosmetics Inc. Brand Ambassador and Talk Show Host on Touch Talk.

Follow on FB https://www.facebook.com/tyishua

https://toughtalktoday.com/

I SUPPORT HER

Kenesa Bowe

Published Author "Rear View Mirror" MS Criminal Justice & Early Childhood Education. Homelessness & Mental Health Advocate.

FB: https://www.facebook.com/authorkenesabowe

www.kenesabowe.com

Pamela O'Hara

Award-Winning Author "Dark Justice Series" Motivational Speaker & Federal Prison System Reform Advocate.

FB: https://www.facebook.com/darkjusticeseries

www.darkjusticeseries.com

Kaleta Green

Author, Hair Designer & Fashionista

FB: https://www.facebook.com/kaletam1

Tabisha McCoy- Franklin

Majored in Psychology and Special Education & Mental Health Advocate.

FB: https://www.facebook.com/tabishaannquanette.mccoy

I SUPPORT HER

Toni Ferguson

4 H Volunteer Recovery Advocate, Wellness & Mindfulness Coach

FB: https://www.facebook.com/toni.ferguson.522

Rosa Diaz

Caged Bird Publishing (language translator advocate), Prison Reform Advocate, First Lady & Nurse

FB: https://www.facebook.com/rose.diaz.96387189

Made in the USA
Middletown, DE
09 August 2020